Lyle C. Brown

Baylor University

Janet Adamski

Baylor University

Thomas J. Hoffman

St. Mary's University

Study Guide

Practicing Texas Politics

TWELFTH EDITION

Brown/Langenegger/García/Lewis

HOUGHTON MIFFLIN COMPANY   BOSTON NEW YORK

Sponsoring Editor: Katherine Meisenheimer
Editorial Assistant: Kendra Johnson
Editorial Assistant: Melissa L. Mednicov
Production/Design Assistant: Bethany Schlegel
Manufacturing Manager: Florence Cadran
Marketing Manager: Nicola Poser

Printed in the U.S.A.

ISBN: 0-618-31048-7

123456789-QF-07 06 05 04 03

CONTENTS

TO THE STUDENT

This study guide is intended to help you understand the politics of state and local government in Texas. It supplements the twelfth edition of *Practicing Texas Politics* by Brown, Langenegger, García, and Lewis, although it is not a substitute for the text. The study guide has been designed for use in a traditional lecture class or a self-paced course.

Each chapter of the study guide covers a corresponding chapter in *Practicing Texas Politics* and is composed of three parts:

I. Preparing to Study
II. Testing Your Knowledge
III. Applying Your Knowledge

Part I, "Preparing to Study," consists of the following sections:

A. Performance Objectives
B. Overview of the Text
C. Key Terms and Concepts
D. Overview of the Readings

Section A, "Performance Objectives," describes what you should be able to do after you have mastered the material in a chapter of *Practicing Texas Politics*. This section serves as both a preview of what to expect from the chapter and, after you have read the chapter, a helpful review. Section B, "Overview of the Text," which briefly summarizes the main topics, is intended for reading both before and after you study the text. Section C, "Key Terms and Concepts," provides a list of words that have been boldfaced in the text to indicate their importance. Included within parentheses are page numbers where these boldfaced terms and concepts are found. Some of these terms (along with many others) are defined in the glossary of *Practicing Texas Politics*, which is printed immediately preceding the index of that book. If, after studying the text, you are unable to identify these key terms and concepts, you should consult the page referred to in parentheses. Section D, "Overview of the Readings," briefly summarizes the content of each reading. If you examine this section both before and after you study the readings, it will serve as both a preview and a review of each reading.

Part II, "Testing Your Knowledge," is organized as follows:

A. True-False Questions on Text Material
B. True-False Questions on Readings
C. Multiple-Choice Questions on Text Material
D. Multiple-Choice Questions on Readings
E. Completion Questions on Text Material
F. Completion Questions on Readings
G. Essay Questions

After careful study and review of the text and readings, you will be ready for a self-test of your knowledge. Sections A through F present three different kinds of questions—true-false, multiple-choice, and completion (or fill-in-the-blank)—on both text material and readings. Answers to these objective questions are provided at the end of each chapter. If you answer a question incorrectly, you should restudy the page or pages of *Practicing Texas Politics* given in parentheses next to that question. Although the experience of answering all of these questions provides the best measure of your mastery of the chapter, answering every odd-numbered question (or even-numbered question) may achieve the same purpose if you are pressed for time.

Section G consists of essay questions and ranking of states according to data provided in or derived from one or more "How Do We Compare" boxes. Page numbers are given for material that should be most useful in writing each essay. The experience of preparing outlines for some or all of the essays may be sufficient preparation for your instructor's essay examinations.

Part III, "Applying Your Knowledge," has two sections:

A. Outside Readings and Cartoons
B. Internet Research Project

Section A, "Outside Readings and Cartoons," assigns five tasks:

1. Summarizing a magazine article or journal article on Texas politics.
2. Summarizing a chapter in a book on Texas politics.
3. Summarizing a newspaper editorial on Texas politics.
4. Summarizing a newspaper article on Texas politics.
5. Interpreting an editorial cartoon on Texas politics, and explaining why you agree or disagree with the cartoonist's point of view

Section B, "Internet Research Project," involves use of electronic sources. Tips on use of the Internet are provided for the benefit of beginners.

By performing the tasks called for in Part III, you will obtain new knowledge that will supplement what you have learned by studying *Practicing Texas Politics*.

Study the appropriate chapter of *Practicing Texas Politics* before you take the self-test provided in Part II of each study guide chapter. Merely searching the text and readings for answers to self-test questions is not an effective study method. After careful study, however, the self-tests should serve as reliable measures of your mastery of the material.

Pages are perforated so that you can submit parts of the study guide to your instructor or file them with notes and other materials you have collected.

Comments and questions on the study guide are welcome; address them to any one of the co-authors:

Lyle C. Brown and Janet Adamski   Thomas J. Hoffman
Department of Political Science   Department of Political Science
Baylor University   St. Mary's University
P.O. Box 97276   One Camino Santa Maria
Waco, Texas 76798–7276   San Antonio, Texas 78228-8571

L.C.B., J.A, and T.J.H.

CHAPTER ONE

The Environment of Texas Politics

I.   *Preparing to Study*

A.   Performance Objectives

After studying and reviewing the text and readings in this chapter, you will be able to:

1.   Illustrate how public policy is formulated, adopted, and implemented.
2.   Define political culture, and explain how political culture has influenced politics in the Lone Star State.
3.   Describe how the frontier experience helped shape political culture in Texas.
4.   Identify the four principal physical regions of Texas and describe important geographic features of each region.
5.   Describe the origin and development of cattle ranching, cotton farming, and oil production in Texas.
6.   Discuss population growth, distribution, and changes that have accompanied urbanization and metropolitanization in Texas.
7.   Identify the three most numerous racial/ethnic groups in Texas today, and note the size and location of the state's Native-American and Asian-American populations.
8.   Explain how the economy of Texas is influenced by high-tech and biotech research and development, services, agriculture, and trade.
9.   Discuss the importance of the immigration issue for Texans.
10. Identify important environmental, water supply, social, and economic problems facing policymakers in the Lone Star State.
11. Propose new public policies for Texas as the state meets important challenges at the beginning of the twenty-first century.

B.   Overview of the Text (pp. 2–35)

Like the other 49 members of the Federal Union, Texas has land, people, and a state government that makes, enforces, and interprets laws.

1

Political Behavior Patterns (pp. 2–7). As a result of political action, public policy is formulated, adopted, and implemented by government. The shaping of public policy in Texas is affected by the state's political culture and geography. Daniel Elazar has classified Texas's political culture as strongly conservative and individualistic. Because of the traditionalistic influence of the Old South, many Texans have inherited racist attitudes. As a result of their war for independence from Mexico, decades of frontier conflict with Native Americans, range wars, and other forms of violence, Texans became accustomed to struggling for survival and settling disputes by force. Today, new influences in an urbanized society are affecting attitudes and reshaping the state's political culture.

The Land (pp. 7–14). Encompassing about 267,000 square miles of territory, Texas is the second largest state. Because of its size, Texas entered the Union with authorization to subdivide into as many as five states.

Cattle, cotton, and oil emerged at different times as dominant elements in Texas's economy and strongly influenced the state's politics. With dropping oil prices and reduced production in the mid-1980s, Texas experienced a sharp decline in government revenue from this source. Early in the twenty-first century, the oil and natural gas industry accounted for less than 6 percent of the state's economy.

The People (pp. 15–24). Texas had more than 20.8 million inhabitants when the federal census was taken in 2000. This was a 22.8 percent increase over the 1990 population. As a result of urbanization and metropolitanization, less than one-fifth of Texas's counties now have more than four-fifths of the state's people. Population percentages (rounded) for Texas's principal ethnic/racial groups in 2000 were Anglo, 52; Latino, 32; African American, 11; and Asian American, 3. There were less than 70,000 Native Americans. Latinos are Texas's fastest-growing population group.

Searching for New Economic Directions (pp. 24–30). The decline of Texas's petroleum industry in the 1980s dealt a blow to the Texas economy, and the bankruptcy of the Houston-headquarterd Enron Corporation in 2001 resulted in loss of money by investors and loss of jobs by thousands of employees. Nevertheless, growth of the state's high-tech and biotech industries illustrate the state's economic development. From 2001 to 2003, however, many high-tech workers lost their jobs. Texas businesses providing health care, personal services, and commercial services have expanded rapidly; but jobs in these service industries tend to pay lower wages and salaries than jobs with manufacturing companies.

The Lone Star State leads the nation as a producer of beef, wool, mohair, cotton, and grain sorghum. The number of Texas farms and ranches has changed from more than 500,000 to about 230,000 since the 1930s, while the average size of each agricultural unit has increased from 300 acres to approximately 575 acres.

Since the North American Free Trade Agreement (NAFTA) was approved in 1993, U.S. trade with Mexico and Canada has increased. Despite related traffic and pollution problems, NAFTA has resulted in jobs and business opportunities for many Texans. Meanwhile, Mexico continues to be plagued with serious economic and political problems.

Meeting New Challenges: Social and Economic Policy Issues (pp. 30–35). In recent years, the Latino population has increased significantly as a result of an influx of undocumented aliens from Mexico. Although the Immigration Reform and Control Act of 1986 and the Immigration Control and Financial Responsibility Act of 1996 were designed to discourage illegal immigration, undocumented aliens continued to cross the Mexican border in search of employment. After the terrorist attacks on the Pentagon and New York's World Trade Center in 2002, the U.S. Congress passed the Enhanced Border Security and Visa Entry Reform Act of 2002, which strengthens efforts to prevent illegal immigration.

Among other challenges faced by Texans are growing water needs, inadequate environmental protection efforts, failure of schools to educate the state's youth for productive roles in an increasingly competitive world economy, and serious poverty-related social problems.

Looking Ahead (p. 35). Human needs and natural disasters will call for government actions in the years ahead. But Texans must realize that their ability to cope with future problems depends on how well our homes and schools prepare young Texans for global change in the twenty-first century.

C.   Key Terms (with textbook page numbers)

politics (2)	patrón system (6)
government (2)	physical regions (9)
public policy (3)	Gulf Coastal Plains (9)
aliens (3)	Interior Lowlands (10)
political culture (4)	Great Plains (10)
moralistic culture (4)	Basin and Range (10)
individualistic culture (4)	Spindletop Field (13)
traditionalistic culture (4)	Texas Railroad Commission (13)
political inefficacy (4-5)	population shift (16)
frontier experience (5)	urbanization (17)
Jim Crow (6)	suburbanization (17)

metropolitanization (17)
metropolitan statistical area (MSA)
   (17)
primary metropolitan statistical area
   (PMSA) (17)
consolidated metropolitan statistical
   area (CMSA) (17)
Anglo (19)
Latino (19)
African American (21)

Asian American (22)
Native American (23)
high technology (25)
North American Free Trade Agreement (NAFTA) (29)
maquiladora (29)
undocumented alien (31)
Texas Water Development Board
   (TWDB) (32)

D. Overview of the Readings (pp. 41–48)

1.1. "Populating Texas" by Joe Holley (pp. 41–44)

While many people imagine a Texas defined by such icons as cowboys, farmers, and the Texas Rangers, the 2000 census reveals a different picture. A largely urban state today, Texas has been so since the 1950s. As well, it enjoys a population defined by racial and cultural diversity. In addition to its traditional ethnic base of Hispanics with ties to Mexico and African Americans, Texas now has significant populations of Asian Americans and of Hispanics from Central America. Further, as its cities have grown, many Texans have moved from employment in farming and ranching to oil and manufacturing. Thus, a traditional picture of Texas dominated by lonesome prairies and solitary, Anglo cowhands does not reflect the Lone Star state of today.

1.2. "Immigration after 9/11" by Edith Austin and Spencer Franklin (pp. 44–48)

Immigration into the United States has become an even stickier issue since the attacks of September 11, 2001. The federal government allows two types of immigration: unlimited and limited. Unlimited immigration is for immediate relatives of U.S. citizens and returning permanent U.S. residents who have been out of the country for more than one year. In the limited category are family-based immigration, employment-related immigration, and lottery immigration for winners of a lottery open to residents of countries with historically low rates of U.S. immigration. Additionally, there is non-immigrant admission, mainly for tourists and students. Of course others come to the United States illegally. Sharing a border with Mexico, each year Texas receives a large number of immigrants, legal and illegal. Along the Texas-Mexico border, many cities have experienced tremendous growth because of strong cross-border ties. Before 9/11, President George W. Bush and Mexican President Vicente Fox began a serious dialogue about the shared border and immigration issues. Both Texas and the United States now must focus on balancing the opportunities offered by close ties to Mexico through trade and immigration with the need to improve security.

II.   *Testing Your Knowledge*

A.   **True-False Questions on Text Material** (with textbook page numbers)

_____   1.1.   Political actors do not include party activists and government officials. (2)

_____   1.2.   Public policy is formulated, adopted, and implemented by government. (2)

_____   1.3.   Before becoming a part of the United States, Texas was an independent republic. (5)

_____   1.4.   Daniel Elazar identifies Texas's political culture with economic and social conservatism. (5)

_____   1.5.   Before the Civil War, most Anglo Texans owned one or more slaves. (6)

_____   1.6.   There is no evidence of a traditionalistic influence in the political culture of Mexican-American Texans. (7)

_____   1.7.   None of the four Mexican states bordering Texas has a larger area than California. (8)

_____   1.8.   The Ogallala Aquifer provides water for irrigating crops in Texas's Gulf Coastal Plains. (10)

_____   1.9.   Employment in Texas's oil and gas industry has tended to increase since the early 1980s. (13–14)

_____   1.10.   Urbanization features migration of people from rural regions to cities. (17)

_____   1.11.   Native Americans make up approximately 5 percent of the residents of Texas. (18)

_____   1.12.   African Americans first entered Texas with Spanish explorers. (21)

_____   1.13.   In *Fortune* magazine's 2003 listing of the 500 largest corporations in America, none was headquartered in Texas. (24)

_____   1.14.   Before its collapse, Enron was the largest bank in Texas. (25)

_____   1.15.   Most agricultural commodities produced in Texas are processed locally. (28)

_____   1.16.   The Immigration Reform and Control Act of 1986 imposed penalties on employers for knowingly hiring undocumented workers. (31)

_____ 1.17. In 1994, when other states sued the federal government to recover costs resulting from illegal immigration, Texas did not sue. (31)

_____ 1.18. Nearly all Texans can read and write well enough to fill out a simple job application form. (34)

_____ 1.19. Texas ranks near the bottom in a ranking of states according to governmental responses to poverty and social problems. (35)

B.   True-False Questions on Readings (with textbook page numbers)

_____ 1.20. As Texas cities began to sprawl in the 1960s, many residents stopped going to downtown areas to shop or work. (42)

_____ 1.21. In recent yeas, new Texans have come increasingly from Mexico and Central America. (44)

_____ 1.22. Some immigrant visas are issued by the U.S. government through a lottery. (45)

_____ 1.23. A Bush-backed amnesty proposal was criticized by some members of the U.S. Congress who contended that it unfairly discriminated against Mexican immigrants for the benefit of those from Central America. (48)

C.   Multiple-Choice Questions on Text Material (with textbook page numbers)

_____ 1.24. Politics determines "who gets what, when, and how," according to political scientist (2)

   a.   Daniel Elazar.
   b.   Lyle C. Brown.
   c.   Harold Lasswell.
   d.   Joyce A. Langenegger

_____ 1.25. After a bill providing for a state pesticide control program is passed by the Texas Legislature and signed by the governor, the new policy is implemented by (3–4)

   a.   private citizens.
   b.   a state governmental agency.
   c.   the state House of Representatives.
   d.   the state Senate.

_____ 1.26. The foundations of Texas's political culture were laid and developed under the flags of six national governments, including (5)

 a. Holland.
 b. Great Britain.
 c. Belgium.
 d. the Confederate States of America.

_____ 1.27. Texas has a political climate that is very favorable to (6)

 a. labor unions.
 b. radical ideologies.
 c. business.
 d. high government spending for social services.

_____ 1.28. Under terms of the congressional resolution whereby Texas became a state, (8)

 a. up to four additional states could be carved out of Texas and admitted to the Union.
 b. Mexico was authorized to join the Union as a superstate.
 c. Texas's public debt was assumed by the federal government.
 d. slavery was prohibited in Texas.

_____ 1.29. Cattle from Mexico interbred with cattle brought to Texas by Anglo settlers and produced the hardy (11)

 a. Hereford cattle.
 b. longhorn cattle.
 c. Angus cattle.
 d. Brahman cattle.

_____ 1.30. More than half of Texas's annual cotton crop is produced in the (13)

 a. High Plains region of West Texas.
 b. Hill Country west of Austin.
 c. Lower Rio Grande Valley of South Texas.
 d. Blacklands of Central Texas.

_____ 1.31. Employing a half million workers who earned more than $11 billion annually, Texas's petroleum industry reached its peak in the (13)

 a. 1920s.
 b. years of World War II.
 c. years of the Vietnam War.
 d. early 1980s.

_____ 1.32. In the early 1990s, there was a break in the pattern of low oil prices as a result of (14)

    a. the election of President Bill Clinton.

    b. congressional approval of NAFTA.

    c. the Whitewater affair.

    d. the Gulf War.

_____ 1.33. Texas's Loving County is (15)

    a. a sparsely populated county on the New Mexican border.

    b. an urban county that contains Houston and its suburbs.

    c. a poor but densely populated county in the Rio Grande Valley.

    d. a densely populated county on the Louisiana border.

_____ 1.34. Their search for employment and their desire for a higher standard of living have been the moving forces behind the large-scale movement of Texas's African Americans to (22)

    a. other countries where they enjoy greater opportunities.

    b. rural areas of Texas and bordering states.

    c. Houston, Dallas, and other urban areas of Texas.

    d. New York and the New England states.

_____ 1.35. Most of Texas's Native Americans live (24)

    a. in towns and cities.

    b. on the Alabama-Coushatta reservation in East Texas.

    c. on the Tigua reservation in the vicinity of El Paso.

    d. on the Texas-Mexico border near Eagle Pass.

_____ 1.36. Before its collapse, Enron reported inflated profits and reduced debt; and this was done with the assistance of Arthur Anderson, (25)

    a. an accounting firm.

    b. a Dallas bank.

    c. a New York broker.

    d. the Texas comptroller of public accounts.

_____ 1.37. A highly-publicized merger of high-tech companies in 2002 involved Compaq and (26)

    a. IBM.

    b. Hewlett-Packard.

    c. Dell.

    d. Apple.

_____ 1.38. Molly Ivins points out that the service sector creates jobs but that this employment (27)

    a.   requires graduate school education.
    b.   is offered only in rural areas.
    c.   is threatened by NAFTA.
    d.   provides low pay.

_____ 1.39. Compared with other states, Texas ranks first in (33)

    a.   per capita spending on air quality.
    b.   per capita spending on water quality.
    c.   water-quality planning.
    d.   toxic air emissions.

_____ 1.40. The ratio of Texas children living in poverty and the total for number of children in the state is (34)

    a.   1 to 5.
    b.   1 to 10.
    c.   1 to 15.
    d.   1 to 20.

D.   Multiple-Choice Questions on Readings (with textbook page numbers)

_____ 1.41. Between 1990 and 2000, the population of Texas increased by nearly (41)

    a.   4 million.
    b.   6 million.
    c.   8 million.
    d.   12 million.

_____ 1.42. A characteristic of Texas counties currently undergoing tremendous population growth is (42)

    a.   nearby oil and gas fields.
    b.   closeness to large cities.
    c.   numerous farms and ranches.
    d.   nearness to the Texas-Oklahoma border.

_____ 1.43. A non-immigrant is an alien admitted to the United States for a specific purpose and (45)

    a.   a fixed wage or salary.
    b.   residence in a designated state.
    c.   limited freedom of travel.
    d.   a limited period of time.

_____   1.44. According to data provided by the U.S. Census Bureau and the Bureau
                   of Labor Statistics, the second-ranking country of birth for illegal im-
                   migrants to the United States is (47)

   a. Canada.
   b. El Salvador.
   c. Guatemala.
   d. Haiti.

E.   Completion Questions on Text Material (with textbook page numbers)

1.45. Values are allocated when a state or local government formulates, adopts, and im-
       plements a _____ policy. (2)

1.46. Attitudes, habits, and general behavior patterns that shape a state's politics are
       parts of its _____ culture. (4)

1.47. Daniel Elazar identifies the Lone Star State's politics with distrust of political
       _____. (5)

1.48. Daniel Elazar insists that the traditionalist influence of the Old
       _____ lingers in Texas. (6)

1.49. The _____ system of certain areas of South Texas features a protecting
       political boss. (7)

1.50. Texas's large area and geographic diversity have created strong
       _____ interests. (7–8)

1.51. Before the _____ War, when slave labor was available, cotton pro-
       duction spread in Texas. (13)

1.52. Texas experienced its first oil boom after the _____ Field was devel-
       oped near Beaumont in 1901. (13)

1.53. From 1987 to 1989, more Texas financial institutions failed than at any time since
       the Great _____. (14)

1.54. The U.S. Census Bureau estimated that about 3.3 million Americans were
       _____ by census takers in 2000. (15)

1.55. Demographer Steven H. Murdock and his associates at Texas A&M University
       have prepared alternative scenarios for _____ growth in Texas. (16)

1.56. A significant number of _____ immigrants established settlements in
       the Hill Country west and north of San Antonio before the Civil War. (19)

1.57. Most of Texas's Asian Americans have immigrated to the United States from _____ Asia. (22)

1.58. In the last two decades, biotechnology-related jobs have increased _____ times faster than the overall increase of employment in Texas. (26)

1.59. Hospitals, nursing homes, hotels, restaurants, bowling alleys, and data processing companies are part of Texas's growing _____ industry. (27)

1.60. Gross income from the products of Texas agriculture amounts to about $_____ billion annually. (28)

1.61. The country that is the largest purchaser of Texas farm and ranch products is _____. (28)

1.62. Today, Mexico has a _____ of about 100 million. (28)

1.63. In the 1990s, the Mexican states of Chiapas, Oaxaca, and Guerrero became the scenes of armed _____. (30)

1.64. Since Texas became part of the Federal Union, the source of many immigration problems has been the border with _____. (30)

1.65. All undocumented aliens must live and work in fear of arrest and _____. (31)

1.66. In 1994, President Bill Clinton appointed former U.S. Representative Barbara Jordan to chair the Commission on _____ Reform. (31)

1.67. Pollution of the Gulf of _____ has resulted in declining catches of fish and shrimp from gulf waters. (33)

1.68. One-_____ of Texas's teachers quit teaching each year. (34)

F.   Completion Questions on Readings (with textbook page numbers)

1.69. The official 2000 census underscores the fact that Texas is truly an _____ state. (41)

1.70. According to Steven Murdock, Texas Anglos are settling in the state's _____ while Hispanics and African Americans are settling in its central cities. (44)

1.71. Economic ties between the United States and Mexico have been strengthened by the North American Free _____Agreement. (47)

1.72.   According to Mexican President Vicente Fox, _____ percent of his country-
men living in the United States earn more, collectively, than all of those living in
Mexico. (48)

G.   Essay Questions (with textbook page numbers)

1.   Write an essay entitled "Texas's Political Culture and the Impact of the Frontier Experience." (5–7)
2.   Identify and describe Texas's four principal physical regions. (9–11)
3.   Describe the importance of cattle, cotton, and oil in the economic development of Texas. (11–14)
4.   Describe Texas's principal demographic features, noting population distribution, urbanization, and metropolitanization. (15–18)
5.   Identify the five most numerous racial/ethnic groups in Texas, and describe
their origins and current geographic distributions. Comment on ways in which
recent migration and immigration have affected the sizes of these groups.
(18–24)
6.   Describe recent developments in Texas agriculture, high technology, biotech-
nology, services, and trade as the Lone Star State has searched for new economic directions. (24–30)
7.   Explain why immigration, water, and environmental protection are important
issues in Texas. (30–33)
8.   Determine the population density for each of the 12 states in the How Do We
Compare boxes at the top of pages 8 and 16 of this chapter. Divide population
by area to find the number of people per square mile. Rank the states from the
most densely populated to the least densely populated.

III. Applying Your Knowledge

A.   Outside Readings and Cartoons

1.   From the endnotes for this chapter or from the updated bibliography of selected sources accessible through the Houghton Mifflin Political Science
home page (politicalscience.college.hmco.com), choose a magazine or journal
article and write a summary of it.
2.   From the endnotes for this chapter or from the updated bibliography of selected sources accessible through the Houghton Mifflin Political Science
home page (politicalscience.college.hmco.com), choose a book and write a
summary of one of its chapters.

3. In a Texas newspaper, find an editorial that relates to the environment of Texas politics. Summarize that editorial, and explain why you agree or disagree with the writer's point of view.

4. Find a newspaper article concerning the environment of Texas politics. Summarize the article, and describe what you do and/or do not like about this piece of reporting.

5. Interpret one of this chapter's cartoons (or another cartoon concerning the environment of Texas politics), and explain why you agree or disagree with the cartoonist's point of view.

6. Explore two or more of the web sites listed among sources for this chapter. Then select one site and write a brief note outlining how its information contributes to your understanding of the environment of Texas politics.

B. Internet Research Project

Objectives

1. To familiarize students with the information available from the Texas State Data Center.
2. To enhance student awareness of changing demographic patterns in their area as well as statewide.
3. To introduce students to the concept of Uniform Resource Locators (URLs).
4. To introduce students to the use of hyperlinks.

URL. http://txsdc.tamu.edu

Description of the Site. The Texas State Data Center is located in the Department of Rural Sociology at Texas A&M University in College Station. The center's primary responsibility is to improve access to census data by researchers and others. It is part of a network of more than 50 centers across the nation, including Puerto Rico and the Virgin Islands. Center personnel provide annual population estimates on a regional (council of governments), MSA (metropolitan statistical area), county, place, and statewide basis. This information is helpful for budget-planning purposes at all levels of government as well as aiding governments and businesses in projecting service needs and consumer markets.

The center also has a population projection program. Every two to three years, projections are revised to predict the Lone Star State's population trends from 1990 to 2040. These studies anticipate many changes in the demography (or population characteristics) of Texas over the first four decades of the twenty-first century. To support its goals, the center publishes reports, conducts workshops, and maintains electronic data at its web site. For this exercise, you will need to use hyperlinks and scroll to obtain information.

The internet is a dynamic, ever-changing environment. If any of the links or instructions needs to be adjusted, consult the textbook's web site for updates of this exercise (http://college.hmco.com/polisci/brown/prac_tex_pol/12e/students/index.html).

Use of Information. Following are the instructions for using this web site (http://txsdc.tamu.edu) to complete the exercise.

1. Once at the web site, go to the top of the screen and click on the button Subjects A to Z. Then go to P (Population and Population Change). Locate the title "Population and Population Change 1980–1990 and 1990–2000." Click on the <u>County</u> link.

2. If you are a Texan, select your home county; otherwise, select the county where your college or university is located. The name of your selected county is _____ County. Fill in the population of this county in 1980 (_____), 1990 (_____), and 2000 (_____). The county's percentage of population change from 1980–1990 was _____ percent and from 1990–2000 was _____ percent.

3. Indicate whether the population of your selected county increased or decreased from 1980–1990 (_____) and from 1990–2000 (_____).

4. Go back to Subjects A to Z (Population and Population Change) to obtain statewide data. Open the document Total Population and Components of Population Change in Texas, 1950–2000. Click on the <u>Texas</u> link. Fill in the percentage for population change in Texas from 1990–2000 (_____).
   a. How does your selected county's percentage of population change (1990–2000) compare to that of the state of Texas for the same period?
   _____

   b. In Texas, the 1990–2000 population change due to natural increase (births minus deaths) was _____ and due to net migration (persons entering minus persons leaving) was _____.

5. Back out of the document, and use the Home link on the top of the page. Click on the link "Texas counties with corresponding COG, Economic Region, Metropolitan Status, and MSA." Your selected county is _____ County. The name of your Council of Government (COG) is

   _____.

6. Click on the "Back" icon at the top of the screen to return to the "Home" page. Go to "The Texas Challenge in the Twenty-First Century report and summary" by following the link. Under "Council of Government Regions

(COGs) Tables," click on "Population for the State of Texas and Council of Government Regions in Texas in 2000 and Projections to 2040. Assuming Alternative Projection Scenarios." Table 2.7 has columns with population data for Anglos, Blacks, Hispanics, and Others.

Find your COG (use the find feature on the Edit button of your browser, or scroll down). There are several tables of population projections. You will be using the first table (SCENARIO 0.0), which assumes a rate of zero net migration into your COG), and the third table (SCENARIO 1.0), which assumes that migration continues at the same rates for all racial and ethnic groups as for the years 1990–2000. Assuming zero net migration (SCENARIO 0.0), the population of your COG in 2040 will be

_____.

7. Assuming zero net migration, rank your COG's racial/ethnic groups from largest to smallest in 2040.

_____

8. Assuming migration continues at the same rate as for years 1990–2000 (SCENARIO 1.0), the population of your COG in 2040 will be

_____.

9. Assuming migration continues at the same rate for years 1990–2000, rank your COGs racial/ethnic groups from largest to smallest in 2040.

_____

Internet Research Tip. When using the Internet, it is helpful to have the address or URL (the Uniform Resource Locator) of a web site. The URL contains several pieces of information. For the site you have been using, the URL can be explained as follows:

1. The http:// stands for hypertext transfer protocol and identifies this page as a part of the Internet.
2. The txsdc.tamu.edu names the server. In this example, the page is identified as being served by the Texas State Data Center (txsdc) and as a part of Texas A&M University (tamu). The .edu identifies Texas A&M as a U.S. university. This site is not served by the World Wide Web.
3. A URL will never end with a period. If you see a URL with a period at the end, do not use the period. It is only there to punctuate a sentence. Likewise, do not use the left arrow (<) and right arrow (>) or parentheses that may enclose a URL.

You have used hyperlinks to move from one page to another in this exercise. Hyperlinks are clickable icons (pictures) or text in a document that are connected to other documents. Typically, if a hyperlink is in text, it will be in a different color from the rest of the text and underlined. As you move the cursor onto the hyperlink, a hand will appear and alert you to the presence of the hyperlink. The URL of the hyperlink will also be displayed at the bottom of your computer screen.

Answers

True-False: Text		Multiple-Choice: Text			
1.1.	F	1.24.	c	1.47.	parties
1.2.	T	1.25.	b	1.48.	South
1.3.	T	1.26.	d	1.49.	patrón
1.4.	T	1.27.	c	1.50.	regional
1.5.	F	1.28.	a	1.51.	Civil
1.6.	F	1.29.	b	1.52.	Spindletop
1.7.	T	1.30.	a	1.53.	Depression
1.8.	F	1.31.	d	1.54.	missed
1.9.	F	1.32.	d	1.55.	population
1.10.	T	1.33.	a	1.56.	German
1.11.	F	1.34.	c	1.57.	Southeast
1.12.	T	1.35.	a	1.58.	four
1.13.	F	1.36.	a	1.59.	services
1.14.	F	1.37.	b	1.60.	14
1.15.	F	1.38.	d	1.61.	Mexico
1.16.	T	1.39.	d	1.62.	population
1.17.	F	1.40.	a	1.63.	rebellion
1.18.	F			1.64.	Mexico
1.19.	T			1.65.	deportation

Multiple-Choice: Readings

1.66. Immigration
1.67. Mexico
1.68. fifth

True-False: Readings

1.20.	T	1.41.	a
1.21.	T	1.42.	b
1.22.	T	1.43.	d
1.23.	F	1.44.	b

Completion: Readings

1.69. urban
1.70. suburbs
1.71. Trade
1.72. 9

Completion: Text

1.45. public
1.46. political

CHAPTER TWO

Federalism and the Texas Constitution

I. *Preparing to Study*

A. Performance Objectives

After studying and reviewing the text and readings in this chapter, you will be able to:

1. Identify provisions of the U.S. Constitution concerning limitations on the states, guarantees to the states, and state powers.
2. Identify provisions of the U.S. Constitution concerning relations among the states.
3. Describe federal-state relations as an evolving process.
4. Describe the historical developments under which each of Texas's state constitutions was written, especially the Constitution of 1876.
5. Trace the steps in the constitutional amendment process from legislative action to gubernatorial proclamation, and describe recent constitutional amendment proposals.
6. List the principal events involved in the unsuccessful constitutional revision efforts in Texas between 1971 and 1975.
7. Summarize important details and provisions of today's Texas Constitution.
8. Describe attempts at constitutional reform through piecemeal constitutional amendments, and address the problem of turnout for voting on proposed constitutional amendments.
9. Suggest provisions that you believe should be included in legislative, executive, and judicial articles for a new Texas Constitution.

B. Overview of the Text (pp. 50-73)

The current Texas Constitution was adopted more than 125 years ago. With many amendments since 1876, it continues to be one major source of the state government's policymaking power. The other major source is membership in the Federal Union.

The American Federal Structure (pp. 50-55). The American federal system involves a division of powers between the national and state governments. The national supremacy clause of the U.S. Constitution stipulates that state constitutions are subject to the U.S. Constitution and state judges are bound by provisions of that document and by the laws and treaties of the national government. Article IV of the U.S. Constitution includes a list of guarantees to the states (for example, territorial integrity, protection against invasion and rebellion, a republican form of government, and equal representation in the U.S. Senate). Also included in this article are provisions concerning relations among states (such as equal privileges and immunities to be recognized for each other's citizens, full faith and credit to be given to each other's public acts and records, and extradition of fugitives who flee from one state to another).

The men who wrote the U.S. Constitution sought to establish machinery for a workable and enduring balance of powers between the national government in Washington and the state governments. Nevertheless, maintaining the Federal Union is an evolving process. Through grants of money, the national government has induced the states to participate in many of its programs.

The Texas Constitution: Politics of Policymaking (pp. 55-63). Texans have been governed under seven constitutions. The Constitution of Coahuila y Tejas, which became effective in 1828, marked Texas's first experience with a state constitution. Eight years later, Texans declared their independence from Mexico, adopted the Constitution of the Republic of Texas, and voted to join the United States. A new state constitution was written in 1845 and approved by Texas voters in 1846 at the same time that they voted to accept a U.S. congressional invitation to join the Federal Union. Three more state constitutions were adopted during the 1860s, when Texas cast its lot with the Confederate States of America (1861), sought reinstatement in the Federal Union (1866), and conformed to the Reconstruction program of the Radical Republicans (1869).

Drafted in the summer of 1875 and adopted in 1876, the current Texas Constitution reflects the slogan of "retrenchment and reform" that was voiced by its framers. They were determined to undo the Reconstruction policies and create a government with strictly limited power. Because of its restrictiveness and detail, more than 400 amendments have been added.

These numerous amendments have caused the Texas Constitution to become excessively long, badly organized, structurally confusing, and unduly detailed. Although some amendments concern constitutional issues of fundamental importance, others deal with matters that should be resolved by statutory law. As a result, large numbers of qualified voters do not bother to vote on proposed amendments.

The Amendment Process (pp. 63-64). Proposal of an amendment requires a joint resolution which must be approved by two-thirds of the membership of each house of the Texas Legislature. Adoption is achieved by a simple majority vote by the electorate in a regular or special election.

There have been unsuccessful efforts in the Texas Legislature to propose a constitutional amendment that would authorize initiative and referendum procedures, which are used in 24 other states. The initiative process permits individuals and groups to submit proposed laws and constitutional amendments to a direct popular vote, whereas a referendum allows them to challenge and overturn laws passed by state legislatures.

Constitutional Revision (pp. 64-69). There have been several attempts to revise the Constitution of 1876. The most important effort involved an amendment, adopted in 1972, establishing a six-member study committee. This committee appointed the 37-member Constitutional Revision Commission that produced a draft proposal for a new constitution in which the Bill of Rights would remain unchanged. The proposal was considered in 1974 by the 63rd Legislature, sitting as a constitutional convention. After the convention failed by three votes to approve a proposed constitution, the 64th Legislature submitted a new constitution to Texas voters in the form of eight separate propositions, or amendments. In an election held on November 4, 1975, all of these propositions were rejected by overwhelming majorities. In 1999, Senator Bill Ratliff and Representative Rob Junell introduced their draft of a proposed constitution in the 76th Legislature. It was not given serious consideration, but piecemeal revision by amendment has continued.

The Texas Constitution: A Summary (pp. 69-73). There are 17 articles in the Texas Constitution. Included in Article I, the Bill of Rights, are guarantees of freedom of speech, press, religion, assembly, and petition. These freedoms are also protected by the Bill of Rights of the U.S. Constitution, but the Texas Constitution is more protective of some rights. The three branches of government are the subjects of Article III (legislative), Article IV (executive), and Article V (judicial). Article VI concerns voting and elections. It establishes voter qualifications, provides for voter registration, and governs the conduct of elections. Various articles, including Article IX (counties) and Article XI (municipalities) provide for the structures and powers of units of local government. Special districts are authorized by an amendment added in 1904. The nine remaining articles are titled Education, Taxation and Revenue, Railroads, Private Corporations, Spanish and Mexican Land Titles (text deleted by an amendment), Public Land and Land Office, Impeachment, General Provisions (the longest article, which covers miscellaneous subjects), and Mode of Amendment.

Looking Ahead (pp. 64–65). Many more constitutional amendments may be expected in the future, unless a new constitution is proposed and adopted. Meanwhile, the organization and powers of state and local governments will continue to be controlled by Texas's much-amended, nineteenth-century constitution.

C.   Key Terms (with textbook page numbers)

Tenth Amendment (50)	constitutional history of Texas (57)
national supremacy clause (51)	Constitution of 1876 (59)
delegated powers (51)	policymaking by constitutional amend-
implied powers (51)	ment (62)
Texas v. *White* (51)	initiative (64)
constitutional guarantees (52)	referendum (64)
privileges and immunities (52)	Constitutional Revision Commission (66)
full faith and credit clause (53)	Constitutional Convention of 1974 (66)
reserved power (53)	Bill of Rights (70)
federal grant-in-aid (54)	Texas Equal Rights Amendment (71)
devolution (54)	separation of powers (71)
block grant (55)	suffrage (72)
preamble (55)	local government (72)

D.   Overview of the Readings (pp. 68-75)

2.1.   "Governor Had to be Poll-Axed" by Kent Biffle (pp. 77-79)

Gubernatorial transitions in Texas have been much less dramatic since the ruckus witnessed in January 1874. After an election, incumbent Governor Edmund J. Davis had to be forced to leave the Capitol. When he stood down after holding out for four days, Davis left his office locked and took the key. Therefore, Governor-elect Coke had to have the door opened with an ax. This stands in sharp contrast to the peaceful transition between the president-elect George W. Bush and his gubernatorial successor, Lieutenant Governor Rick Perry, on December 24, 2000.

2.2.   "Of Rutabagas and Redeemers: Rethinking the Texas Constitution of 1876" by Patrick G. Williams (pp. 79-84)

A myth of the Texas Constitutional Convention of 1876 is that the resulting constitution was largely the work of members of the Texas Patrons of Husbandry, informally known as the Grange. The myth continues that these farmers were most interested in a small state government with limited powers. Finally, Grangers have been credited with defeating a proposed poll tax, a tool often used by former Confederate states to disenfranchise African Americans. As the author demonstrates, however, the true story of the convention is much more complex. In fact, the Democrats who made up most of the convention were divided along a number of lines, not just into Grange and non-Grange delegations. A more careful examination of historical records is needed to help us demythologize the making of the Constitution of 1876.

2.3. "Hermine Tobolowsky: Mother of Texas's Equal Legal Rights Amendment" by Tai Kreidler (pp. 84-88).

Hermine Tobolowsky deserves much credit for her efforts leading to the addition of the Equal Legal Rights Amendment (ELR) to the Texas Constitution and the enactment of laws meant to ensure gender equality. Tobolowsky, with the active support of the Texas Federation of Business and Professional Women's Clubs (BPW), spent decades overcoming the opposition of Texas legislators to women's equal legal rights. Finally, with bills passed in the 1965 legislative session, adoption of the ELR Amendment by the legislature, and popular approval of this amendment at the polls in 1972, Tobolowsky saw the realization of many of her goals of gender equality in Texas.

II. *Testing Your Knowledge*

A. True-False Questions on Text Material (with textbook page numbers)

_____ 2.1. American federalism has been described by North Carolina's former governor Terry Sanford as "a system of states within a state." (50)

_____ 2.2. The Tenth Amendment to the U.S. Constitution refers to powers reserved to the states. (50)

_____ 2.3. The framers of the U.S. Constitution intended to create a governmental system whereby the states could dominate the national government. (51)

_____ 2.4. If the government of the state of Texas were to deny an African-American citizen the right to vote on the basis of race, that act would violate the U.S. Constitution. (51)

_____ 2.5. Within the U.S. constitutional system, the reserved powers of the states are clearly defined. (53)

_____ 2.6. The Civil War pitted the North against the South in a struggle to settle the issue of states' rights versus national supremacy regarding slavery. (54)

_____ 2.7. Policymaking by the states has not been influenced by grants of money from the U.S. government. (54)

_____ 2.8.   Political scientists and legal scholars generally believe that constitution makers should not try to solve policy problems but should establish clearly the process for solving them. (55)

_____ 2.9.   Texas's seventh constitution has been amended more than 400 times. (55)

_____ 2.10. The Texas Constitutions of 1861, 1866, and 1869 were necessitated by the Civil War and Reconstruction. (58)

_____ 2.11. When adopted in 1876, the Texas Constitution required voter registration. (60)

_____ 2.12. The Texas Constitution of 1876 is famed for its brevity and logical organization. (61)

_____ 2.13. Statutory detail in the Texas Constitution of 1876 has led to many constitutional amendments. (61)

_____ 2.14. During the Texas constitutional convention of 1974, Governor Dolph Briscoe intervened aggressively for the purpose of supporting needed constitutional reform. (66)

_____ 2.15. The Texas constitutional convention of 1974 failed to adopt a draft constitution for submission to the state's voters. (66)

_____ 2.16. In 1975, the Texas Legislature proposed a constitutional revision resolution composed of ten articles in eight sections. (66)

_____ 2.17. Less than 25 percent of Texas's registered voters participated in the special election that rejected the constitution proposed in 1975. (67)

_____ 2.18. In 1999, Senator Bill Ratliff and Representative Rob Junell introduced a draft constitution for consideration by the 76th Legislature. (67)

_____ 2.19. With regard to all rights, the Texas Constitution is less protective than the U.S. Constitution. (70)

_____ 2.20. The U.S. Congress, the U.S. Supreme Court, and amendments to the U.S. Constitution have diminished state governmental power over the conduct of elections. (72)

B.   True-False Questions on Readings (with textbook page numbers)

_____ 2.21. When Texas Governor Edmund Jackson Davis lost his bid for reelection, his first reaction was to give up his office. (77)

_____ 2.22. Before the governorship passed from George W. Bush to Rick Perry, Texas was without a governor for less than a day. (77)

_____ 2.23. The "Rutabagas" were constitutional convention delegates who proclaimed their membership in the Ku Klux Klan. (80)

_____ 2.24. According to historian Patrick G. Williams, the Granger delegates to the constitutional convention of 1875 always voted as a bloc. (81)

_____ 2.25. Hermine Tobolowsky is considered as the "mother" of the Texas Equal Legal Rights Amendment (84)

_____ 2.26. The Texas Federation of Business and Professional Women's Clubs opposed adoption of the Texas Equal Legal Rights Amendment. (85)

C.   Multiple-Choice Questions on Text Material (with textbook page numbers)

_____ 2.27. Under the U.S. Constitution, the national government's authority to regulate interstate and foreign commerce, to coin money, and to declare war are examples of (51)

    a. implied powers.
    b. inherent powers.
    c. delegated powers.
    d. reserved powers.

_____ 2.28. Rights of Texans to enter and leave Oklahoma, to sue in the courts of Oklahoma, and to own property in Oklahoma are guaranteed by the U.S. Supreme Court's interpretation of the U.S. Constitution's provisions concerning (52)

    a. natural law.
    b. interstate commerce.
    c. suffrage.
    d. privileges and immunities.

_____ 2.29. Police powers, taxing powers, and power of eminent domain are examples of the states' (53)

    a. reserved powers.
    b. implied powers.
    c. inherent powers.
    d. enumerated powers.

_____ 2.30. When it went into effect in 1876, the Texas Constitution had about (55)

    a. 28,600 words.
    b. 50,500 words.
    c. 63,000 words.
    d. 110,000 words.

_____ 2.31. Many of the constitutional convention delegates elected in 1875 were members of the Texas Grange, which was (59)

    a. representative of Texas's urban population.
    b. supportive of the policies of the Davis administration.
    c. representative of big-business interests.
    d. committed to the cause of economy and limited government.

_____ 2.32. Over the last century, most amendments to the Texas Constitution have dealt with policy issues that should have been resolved by (61)

    a. executive orders issued by the governor.
    b. the legislature.
    c. litigation in state courts.
    d. opinions of the U.S. Supreme Court.

_____ 2.33. The Texas Constitution establishes an amendment process that features actions (63)

    a. first by the governor and then by the Supreme Court of Texas.
    b. first by the House of Representatives and then by the Senate.
    c. first by the Legislature and then by the voters.
    d. by the Legislature in two successive regular sessions.

_____ 2.34. In 1971, the 62nd Texas Legislature began the constitutional revision process by proposing an amendment authorizing a convention composed of (64)

    a. members of the 63rd Legislature.
    b. delegates chosen by the voters in a special election.
    c. members of the Constitutional Revision Commission.
    d. members of the 62nd Legislature and all of Texas's representatives and senators serving in the U.S. Congress.

_____ 2.35. The function of the Constitutional Revision Commission was to (66)

    a. revise the constitution proposed by the Texas Legislature.
    b. propose amendments to the Constitution of 1876.
    c. prepare a draft constitution for submission to the Texas Legislature.
    d. publicize the constitution proposed by the legislative constitutional convention.

_____ 2.36. The constitutional document submitted to Texas voters in November 1975 (66)

    a. was composed 10 articles in eight separate propositions or sections.

    b. differed very little from the Constitution of 1876.

    c. required voters to cast a single vote for approval or rejection of the document.

    d. contained 26 articles.

_____ 2.37. Originally included in the constitutional revision package submitted to Texas voters in 1975 and adopted in 1979 as a constitutional amendment is the authorization allowing (68)

    a. restricted gubernatorial removal power over appointed statewide officials.

    b. execution of convicted murderers by hanging.

    c. reduction of the number of counties.

    d. adoption of the Missouri Plan for selecting state judges.

_____ 2.38. The first article of the Texas Constitution concerns (70)

    a. voting qualifications and the administration of elections.

    b. organization and functions of political parties.

    c. organization and powers of the executive branch.

    d. protections for people and property against arbitrary governmental actions.

D. Multiple-Choice Questions on Readings (with textbook page numbers)

_____ 2.39. Governor E. J. Davis lost his bid for reelection to (77)

    a. Rick Perry.

    b. George W. Bush.

    c. Richard Coke.

    d. Sam Houston.

_____ 2.40. Governor E. J. Davis claimed that the results of the election of 1873 were invalid because of a controversial (77-78)

    a. semicolon.

    b. colon.

    c. comma.

    d. period.

_____ 2.41. More than 40 percent of the delegates to the Texas constitutional convention of 1876 were members of the (81)

    a. Anglican Church.
    b. Patrons of Husbandry.
    c. Texas Rangers.
    d. Republican Party.

_____ 2.42. What statement best describes the convention delegates who voted to prohibit inclusion of a poll tax in the Texas Constitution of 1876? (82)

    a. They came from majority white counties that voted solidly Democratic.
    b. They were long-time members of the Grange.
    c. They were African Americans.
    d. They had fought in the ranks of the Union Army during the Civil War.

_____ 2.43. Hermine Tobolowsky was a (85)

    a. lawyer.
    b. rancher.
    c. teacher.
    d. nurse.

_____ 2.44. In November 1972, supporters of the Texas Equal Legal Rights Amendment outvoted their opponents by a ratio of nearly (88)

    a. 14 to 1.
    b. 10 to 1.
    c. 4 to 1.
    d. 2 to 1.

E. **Completion Questions on Text Material** (with textbook page numbers)

2.45. Under the U.S. Constitution, the national government's _____ powers are most clearly linked to the "necessary and proper" clause of Article 1. (51)

2.46. Among the members of Congress representing Texas, a total of _____ are members of the U.S. Senate. (52)

2.47. Persons from Texas who are visiting in another state are entitled to all of the privileges and _____ to which citizens of that state are entitled. (52)

2.48. Under the extradition provision of the U.S. Constitution, a person committing a crime in Texas before fleeing to Oklahoma should be _____ to Texas authorities if requested by the governor of Texas. (53)

2.49. In response to the Great Depression of the 1930s, Congress increased financial assistance to the states through federal _____ programs. (54)

2.50. In 1836, the Republic of Texas was created after a declaration of independence from _____. (57)

2.51. Under the Texas Constitution of 1869, the Radical Republicans gained control of the legislature and elected E. J. Davis as _____. (58)

2.52. When the Constitution of 1876 was put to a vote, Texans in the state's largest cities tended to vote _____ it. (60)

2.53. A constitutional amendment adopted in 1999 authorizes garnishment of _____ for support of an ex-spouse as ordered by a court. (61)

2.54. A proposed amendment to the Texas Constitution must be approved by at least 21 senators and _____ representatives in the state legislature. (63)

2.55. Official newspaper publicity for a proposed amendment to the Texas Constitution involves publication of a short _____ statement describing the amendment. (63)

2.56. Entitled "Suffrage," Article VI of the Texas Constitution establishes _____ for voters. (72)

2.57. In its original form, the only type of special district mentioned in the Texas Constitution was the _____ district. (73)

2.58. The text of Article XIII, Spanish and Mexican Land Titles, was _____ by amendment in 1969. (73)

2.59. Article XVI, the longest article in the Texas Constitution, is titled _____ Provisions. (73)

F.   Completion Questions on Readings (with textbook page numbers)

2.60. In the gubernatorial election of 1873, E. J. Davis's opponent outpolled him by a ratio of ____ to 1. (77)

2.61. In an unsuccessful effort to hold onto his office, Texas governor E. J. Davis sought help from Ulysses S. Grant, _____ of the United States. (78)

2.62. The nickname Rutabaga was given to the constitutional convention delegate from Collin County named John _____. (79)

2.63. Framers of the Texas Constitution of 1876 prohibited the state from spending money to promote immigration or construction of _____. (80)

2.64. In her Equal Legal Rights work, Hermine Tobolowsky benefitted from Hyman
_____'s connections with the Retail Merchants Association. (86)

2.65. Senator Wardlaw Lane, an opponent of Equal Legal Rights who had made a re-
mark about "_____ little women," was defeated in his bid for reelection in 1962. (86)

G. Essay Questions (with textbook page numbers)

1. Write an essay entitled "Distribution of Powers Between the Federal and State
Governments Under Provisions of the U.S. Constitution." (50-52)
2. Write an essay entitled "Interstate Relations, State Immunity, and State Powers." (52-54)
3. Write an essay describing the circumstances under which Texas's first three
constitutions were obtained in 1827, 1836 and 1845; and point out significant
features of these constitutions. (57-58)
4. Explain how the experiences of Texans during the Civil War and the era of
Radical Reconstruction influenced some of the original provisions of the Constitution of 1876. (58-60)
5. Write an essay in which you describe the procedure whereby an amendment to
the Texas Constitution is proposed, publicized, and adopted or rejected by the
voters; and comment on the numbers of amendments proposed and adopted
since 1879. (63-65)
6. Write an essay on "Texas's Unsuccessful Constitutional Revision Efforts in
the 1970s and Revision Proposals in the 1990s." (64-68)
7. Some Texans prefer to maintain their state constitution with few or no
changes; others favor piecemeal revision through the amendment process; and
others want a new constitution written by legislators or delegates elected to
form a constitutional convention. Explain which course of action you would
prefer and why. (67-69)
8. Summarize the principal provisions of the Texas Constitution concerning
rights of the people, powers of government, suffrage, and local governments.
(70–73)
9. Rank the 12 states in the How Do We Compare box at the top of page 56 in
this chapter in descending order according to year of adoption; also rank these
states in descending order according to approximate number of words. Is there
an apparent relationship between these rankings.
10. Rank the 12 states in the How Do We Compare box at the bottom of page 62
in this chapter in descending order according to number of amendments since
adoption of the current constitution; also rank these states in descending order
according to average number of amendments per year through 2001. Is there

an apparent relationship between these rankings or with rankings according to approximate number of words?

III. *Applying Your Knowledge*

A.   Outside Readings and Cartoons

1.   From the endnotes for this chapter or from the updated bibliography of selected sources accessible through the Houghton Mifflin Political Science home page (politicalscience.college.hmco.com), choose a magazine or journal article and write a summary of it.
2.   From the endnotes for this chapter or from the updated bibliography of selected sources accessible through the Houghton Mifflin Political Science home page (politicalscience.college.hmco.com), choose a book and write a summary of one of its chapters.
3.   In a Texas newspaper, find an editorial that relates to American federalism or the Texas Constitution. Summarize that editorial, and explain why you agree or disagree with the writer's point of view.
4.   Find a newspaper article concerning American federalism or the Texas Constitution. Summarize the article and describe what you do and/or do not like about this piece of reporting.
5.   Interpret one of this chapter's cartoons (or another cartoon concerning American federalism or the Texas Constitution), and explain why you agree or disagree with the cartoonist's point of view.
6.   Explore two or more of the web sites listed among sources for this chapter. Then select one site and write a brief note outlining how its information contributes to your understanding of federalism and/or the Texas Constitution.

B.   Internet Research Project

Objectives

1.   To increase student understanding of the purposes of the Texas Legislative Reference Library.
2.   To familiarize students with amendments to the Texas Constitution.
3.   To develop an understanding of home pages.

URL. http://www.lrl.state.tx.us

Description of the Site. This site is maintained by the Legislative Reference Library. Established in 1969, the library is an agency of the Texas Legislature. It serves as a reference and research resource for legislators and their staff members, state agency personnel, and the general public. Materials available at the library include books and periodicals related to issues in which legislators are interested, documents from state legislative sessions (such as the daily journals and copies of all printed bills and resolutions), and minutes of all state agency meetings. The library also provides a newspaper clipping service that is used by the authors of Practicing Texas Politics and other researchers.

In addition, the library's web site provides information on bills and resolutions introduced in legislative sessions since 1995, information for conducting research on legislation, and a reference desk with links to many resources. There is also a data base with information concerning proposed amendments to the Texas Constitution from 1876 through the most current legislative session.

The internet is a dynamic, ever-changing environment. If any of the links and instructions need to be adjusted, please consult the textbook's web site for updates of this exercise (http://college.hmco.com/polisci/brown/prac_tex_pol/12e/students/index.html).

Use of Information. Following are the instructions for using the web site of the Legislative Reference Library (http://www.lrl.state.tx.us).

1. Under "Legislative Information," click on the hypertext "Constitutional amendments."

2. Select Legislative Session: 53—R.S. (1953); Article: Any; Adopted. Then click on "View Amendments."
   a. What bill (in this case a House joint resolution) required women to serve on juries? HJR _____
   b. Click on "Details" for that bill. Then, under "Articles affected," click on the number to the right of "Article 16: Amends." What does the word "men" in the Texas Constitution mean when used in reference to grand or petit juries?

3. Back up to the Constitutional Amendments—Search page. Select Legislative Session: 62—R.S. (1971); Article: Any; Adopted. Click on "View Amendments."
   a. What is the number of the Senate joint resolution proposing equal rights for women? SJR _____
   b. What is the proposition number for listing equal rights for women on the ballot? Prop. _____

4. Click on "Details" of SJR 16, Proposition 7, Equal Rights for Women. Under "Articles affected," click on the number to the right of "Article 1: Adds." Then click on the number next to "Articles Affected." As a result of this amendment to the State Constitution, Texas Laws cannot discriminate against individuals for what five reasons? (1) _____, (2) _____, (3) _____, (4) _____, and (5) _____.

5. Go back to "Details" for SJR 16, Proposition 7, Equal Rights for Women. Under "Proposition" obtain the following data: (a) election date (_____), (b) number of votes for adoption (_____), (c) number of votes against adoption (_____).

6. Return to the Constitutional Amendments—Search page. Select Legislative Session: 20—R.S. (1887); Article: Any; Either. Click on View Amendments.
    a. How many amendments were proposed?

        _____

    b. How many amendments were adopted?

        _____

7. Return to the Constitutional Amendments—Search page. Select Legislative Session: 77—R.S. (2001); Article: Any; Either. Click on View Amendments.
    a. How many amendments were proposed?

        _____

    b. How many amendments were adopted?

        _____

8. Return to the Constitutional Amendments—Search page. Select Legislative Session: 78—R.S. (2003); Article: Any; Either. Click on View Amendments.
    a. How many amendments were proposed?

        _____

    b. How many amendments were adopted?

        _____

Internet Research Tip. The first web page of a site is called the home page. If you fail to include the URL for a specific page, the web server most often accesses the site's home page. It contains links to other sites maintained by the web server. As you connect to other pages within the web site, notice that the URL expands to provide the address for the specific web page you are viewing.

Answers

True-False: Text	Multiple-Choice: Text	Completion: Text
2.1. T	2.27. c	2.45. implied
2.2. T	2.28. d	2.46. two
2.3. F	2.29. a	2.47. immunities
2.4. T	2.30. a	2.48. returned
2.5. F	2.31. d	2.49. grant-in-aid
2.6. T	2.32. b	2.50. Mexico
2.7. F	2.33. c	2.51. governor
2.8. T	2.34. a	2.52. against
2.9. T	2.35. c	2.53. wages
2.10. T	2.36. a	2.54. 100
2.11. F	2.37. a	2.55. explanatory
2.12. F	2.38. d	2.56. qualifications
2.13. T		2.57. school
2.14. F		2.58. deleted
2.15. T	**Multiple-Choice: Readings**	2.59. General
2.16. T		
2.17. T	2.39. c	**Completion: Readings**
2.18. T	2.40. a	
2.19. F	2.41. b	2.60. 2
2.20. T	2.42. a	2.61. President
	2.43. a	2.62. Johnson
True-False: Readings	2.44. c	2.63. railroads
		2.64. Tobolowsky
2.21. F		2.65. stupid
2.22. T		
2.23. F		
2.24. F		
2.25. T		
2.26. F		

CHAPTER 3

Local Governments

I.   *Preparing to Study*

A.   Performance Objectives

After studying and reviewing the text and readings in this chapter, you will be able to:

1. Explain the differences between general-law cities and home-rule cities in Texas.
2. Compare the structures of the principal forms of municipal government operating in Texas.
3. Explain the difference between the at-large system and single-member districts for electing council members in Texas cities.
4. List typical public services provided by municipalities in Texas.
5. Describe the sources of revenue for Texas municipalities and illustrate typical expenditures.
6. Describe the structure of and operation of county government, noting the powers and functions of elected county officers.
7. Describe the sources of revenue for Texas counties, and illustrate typical expenditures.
8. Identify two basic problems that underlie reform of county government, and note special problems of the 40 counties on or near the Mexican border.
9. Outline the principal characteristics of independent school districts, junior or community college districts, and noneducation special districts.
10. Summarize the means whereby some of the problems of Texas's metropolitan areas have been addressed.

B.   Overview of the Text (pp. 90–119)

An understanding of grassroots politics is necessary if citizens are to influence policymaking designed to address problems of inner cities, suburbs, or rural areas.

Overview of Grassroots Problems (pp. 90–91). Texas's cities, counties, and special districts must deal with a wide range of issues. Included are the problems of violent crime, narcotics addiction, the AIDS epidemic, decaying roads and bridges, dysfunctional schools, and related environmental and water supply issues like those of the Edwards Aquifer. Consequently, policies made by the governing bodies of local governments affect all citizens. Some Texans become directly involved in local politics by running for city, county, or special-district offices; others limit their participation to voting. But many apathetic citizens do not vote, so they miss important opportunities to influence policymaking in city halls, county courthouses, and special-district offices.

Municipal Governments (pp. 91–103). Texas municipalities are chartered as general-law cities or home-rule cities. A municipality of the latter type must have a population of 5,000 or more at the time its voters choose to become a home-rule city and adopt a charter.

The cities of Texas are organized according to one of the following models: strong mayor-council, weak mayor-council, council-manager, or commission. Each of these forms of municipal corporation includes a popularly elected policymaking body, usually called the city council.

In recent years, municipal politics in Texas has featured rising expectations of African Americans and Latinos for equal representation in city councils. Some of the state's largest cities have implemented single-member district plans for electing all council members, whereas Houston has adopted a plan that combines single-member and at-large election systems. Austin has an electoral system whereby each candidate for the city council files for a place. Council members are then elected on an at-large basis with all voters voting in each place contest. More than 40 Texas cities now use a cumulative voting system that enhances election opportunities for Latinos and African Americans.

Typical concerns of municipal governments include traffic safety, consumer affairs, pollution control, tree preservation, city planning, building safety, annexation of territory, and zoning restrictions. Appointed advisory bodies assist departments in implementing policies. Nevertheless, controversies arise when some services are cut or when new services are added.

Texas cities raise revenue from general property taxes, sales taxes, franchise fees paid by public utilities, licenses for the sale of alcoholic beverages, building and plumbing permits, and money collected by municipal courts in the form of court costs, fines, and forfeitures. Some cities profit from operating water, electric, and gas utilities. Since 2001, cities may ask voters every four years to approve a quarter-cent sales tax (up to a total of 1 per cent) for services or projects such as mass transit, economic development, public safety, and street maintenance. When revenue does not cover expenses, cities borrow money by selling general obligation bonds (redeemed out of a city's property tax revenue) or revenue bonds (redeemed out of revenues from the property or activity financed by the bond sale). Both federal and state governments grant some financial aid to municipalities and other local governmental units. Generally, appropriations by state and federal governments are shrinking as sources for municipal revenue, especially for economic development. Thus, cities must opt for innovative ways to raise revenue for stimulating their local economies.

Counties (pp. 103–112). Texas has 254 counties, but all counties have essentially the same governmental structure. The principal policymaking organ of county government is the county commissioners court. It is a body composed of the county judge and four commissioners elected for four-year terms to represent precincts of approximately equal population. Presided over by the county judge, the commissioners court adopts the county budget, sets the property tax rate, draws boundaries for election precincts, supervises the conduct of elections, and directs the construction and maintenance of county roads and bridges. Major administrative responsibility at the county level is vested in the county judge, who is elected for a term of four years. The county sheriff, attorney, clerk, tax assessor-collector, and treasurer are also elected for four-year terms.

Texas counties rely heavily on property taxes for revenue. They also benefit from fees for alcoholic beverage permits, and they share the state motor fuel tax and motor vehicle registration and certificate-of-title fees. Federal grants-in-aid and borrowing through the sale of bonds provide additional county revenues.

Spending patterns vary from county to county, but maintenance of roads and bridges requires the greatest expenditures by rural counties. Because Texas counties do not have home-rule status, the organization of county governments is dictated by constitutional provisions that are not easily changed. Servicing residents of colonias in the 40 counties on or near the Mexican border presents special problems for county governments.

Special Districts (pp. 112–116). Texas's special districts fall into two basic categories: school districts and noneducation special districts. Special districts are classified as units of government because they have an organized existence, a governmental character, and substantial independence from other units of government.

More than 1,000 independent school districts administer the public schools of Texas. Each independent school district is supervised by a popularly elected board of trustees. Board members set personnel policy, determine wage and salary schedules, provide for building construction and maintenance, select textbooks, and set the property tax rate for the district.

Junior or community college districts provide two-year academic programs beyond high school, along with various technical and vocational programs. Although they receive federal and state funds, these institutions of higher education are partially financed by local property taxes and by tuition and fees paid by students. Each junior or community college district is governed by a popularly elected board that sets the tax rate, issues bonds (subject to voter approval), and adopts an annual budget.

Noneducation special districts in Texas include more than 1,000 water or utility districts and hundreds of housing authorities, water conservation districts, and hospital districts. Mass transit authorities (like Houston's Metro and Dallas's DART) serve seven of the state's largest metropolitan areas.

Metropolitan Areas (pp. 116–118). The problems of local governments in Texas's big-city areas are especially troublesome because of the large number of citizens directly affected. Nevertheless, grassroots governments face challenges everywhere in the Lone Star State. Because of the relatively large number of Texas counties, the proliferation of special districts, and the incorporation of new municipalities, 24 councils of governments (COGs) have been created to promote regional planning and cooperation among units of local government. Despite the fears of some critics who believe that COGs may lead to metro governments, guidelines for federal grants have stimulated the development of these regional councils. Aside from COG services, annexation of adjacent territory is the main device whereby individual cities attempt to deal with metropolitan problems.

Looking Ahead (pp. 118–119). More citizen participation and development of a sense of community are needed to improve the functioning of Texas's cities, counties, and special districts. The problems of central cities are especially critical. Whether newly empowered African-American and Latino voters will make a difference remains to be seen.

C. **Key Terms** (with textbook page numbers)

municipal government (91)
general-law city (92)
home-rule city (92)
ordinance (92)
strong mayor-council form (93)
weak mayor-council form (93)
commission form (96)
council-manager form (96)
term limits (98)
nonpartisan election (98)
at-large district (98)

single-member district (98)
cumulative voting (98)
place system (99)
municipal bond (103)
economic development (103)
tax reinvestment zone (TRZ) (103)
tax abatement (103)
tax increment financing (TIF) (103)
county (103)
commissioners court (104)
Avery v. *Midland County* (104)

county judge (107)	bond (110)
county attorney (108)	colonia (111)
county sheriff (108)	independent school district (ISD) (112)
county clerk (108)	junior college or community college
county tax assessor-collector (108)	district (113)
county tax appraisal district (108)	noneducation special district (115)
county treasurer (109)	council of governments (COG) (116)
county auditor (109)	metro government (118)
county surveyor (109)	

D. Overview of the Readings (pp. 111–120)

3.1. "Accentuating the Positive: How Laura Miller Was Elected Mayor of Dallas with a 'Small Things' Agenda of Change" by Mary Clare Jalonick (pp. 122–125)

On 19 January 2002, Laura Miller finished first in an electoral contest to select a successor to Dallas mayor Ron Kirk. But with only 48.8 percent of the vote, this Dallas city council member and former reporter for the alternative news-weekly *Dallas Observer* fell short of the absolute majority required to capture that office in the first round. A month later, however, she defeated runner-up candidate Tom Dunning, a Dallas businessman and chair of the Dallas/Fort Worth Airport board. Although outspent by Dunning, Miller focused on a need for change in City Hall and "little things" that included parks, roads, swimming pools, and safe neighborhoods. With strong communication skills and a positive message, she tapped into a popular feeling of discontent and won the support of 55 percent of Dallas voters in the February runoff.

3.2. "'Extreme' Term Limits—San Antonio Style" by Alexander E. Briseno (pp. 126–130)

After San Antonio's city council passed a string of unpopular measures in the 1980s, a taxpayers "watchdog" group successfully petitioned for votes on a property-tax rollback, construction of the Applewhite Reservoir, and term limits for members of the city council. One result was a city charter amendment limiting to two the number of terms that the mayor and council members can serve. Alexander Briseno contends that such "extreme" term limits undermine newly elected officials' ability to move through the political cycle: learning, adapting, executing, campaigning, and completing projects. This restriction produces successive groups of new council members who need time to "get up to speed" on the voluminous work of city government. Further, he notes that term limits reduce the pool of political talent available for filling elective offices in San Antonio. As a remedy, Briseno suggests introducing longer terms of office or modifying the term limits now in place.

3.3. "Bottoms Up" by Cecilia Ball (pp. 130–134)

While some observers in Brownsville see the upscale Paseo de la Resaca development as proof of the potential for change along the U.S.-Mexican border, Cecilia Balli points to Cameron Park as a better example of what is possible. Originally, this colonia was an unincorporated area lacking basic services for the impoverished residents who were paying for small plots of land and building their homes piecemeal without professional help. Today, Cameron Park is identified as the poorest place in the United States, based on median income for towns with more than a thousand households. Nevertheless, the colonia's activists have secured assistance from Brownsville, Cameron County, state agencies, the federal government, and private organizations to obtain more social services and better housing. In large part, their success is the result of the residents' own efforts, along with help from local churches and Valley Interfaith, which is a grassroots community group dedicated to improving the quality of life for poor people along the Rio Grande.

II. Testing Your Knowledge

A. True-False Questions on Text Material (with textbook page numbers)

_____ 3.1. It is common to find 90 percent or more of a community's qualified voters participating in a local election. (91)

_____ 3.2. In Texas, a substantial change in the size of a city's population automatically changes its incorporation status. (92)

_____ 3.3. Citizens draft and adopt city charters that establish powers of municipal officers and spell out procedures for passing ordinances. (92)

_____ 3.4. The council-manager form of city government is used in the ten largest cities the United States. (93)

_____ 3.5. The city council of a weak-mayor city may override the mayor's veto. (93)

_____ 3.6. The commission form of city government features a single all-powerful executive official. (96)

_____ 3.7. Among home-rule cities in Texas, the most popular form of government is the council-manager form. (96)

_____ 3.8. Most cities have appointed boards and commissions that work in an advisory capacity with municipal departments that implement ordinances. (100)

_____ 3.9. The general property tax is the only tax Texas cities are allowed to levy. (101)

_____ 3.10. Texas municipalities may levy fees for issuing beer and liquor licenses. (101)

_____ 3.11. The Texas Constitution prohibits municipalities from making profits on city-owned gas and electric utility systems. (102)

_____ 3.12. Revenue bonds are redeemed out of revenue from the property or activities financed by sale of the bonds. (102)

_____ 3.13. Under Texas law, a municipality may reduce the tax burden on homeowners by granting a homestead exemption. (102)

_____ 3.14. Municipalities may create tax reinvestment zones (TRZs) through temporary tax abatement. (103)

_____ 3.15. Each Texas county has approximately the same number of people. (104)

_____ 3.16. Policymaking in Texas county government is performed mainly by a body called the commissioners court. (104)

_____ 3.17. As mandated by the U.S. Supreme Court, each Texas county must be divided into commissioner precincts of substantially equal population. (104)

_____ 3.18. The county judge presides over meetings of the commissioners court in Texas counties. (107)

_____ 3.19. In the 2002 general election, Bexar County was the last county in the country to count its votes because of a complicated two-page ballot. (108)

_____ 3.20. After George W. Bush was elected president of the United States, the property taxes on his ranch near Crawford were reduced to less than $100. (109)

_____ 3.21. Under terms of the Texas Constitution, county governments have complete control over their spending. (111)

_____ 3.22. Texas's public junior or community colleges enroll more than 70 percent of the state's freshmen and sophomores. (113)

_____ 3.23. Special districts may be created to provide public services that cannot be undertaken by Texas municipalities and counties because of state constitutional restrictions. (115)

B. **True-False Questions on Readings** (with textbook page numbers)

_____ 3.24. As a member of the Dallas city council, Laura Miller antagonized the mayor and many of the city's powerful leaders. (123)

_____ 3.25. Tom Dunning, Laura Miller's strongest opponent in Dallas's 2002 mayoral election, was backed by business leaders in north Dallas and African-American voters in south Dallas. (124)

_____ 3.26. Contributing to instigation of term limits in San Antonio were city budgets that reduced service levels while raising the property tax rate. (126)

_____ 3.27. Reelection campaigns for San Antonio's city council members seldom last longer than one month. (128)

_____ 3.28. A typical colonia along the Texas-Mexico border is an unincorporated neighborhood lacking paved streets, water and electricity hookups, and sewer lines. (131)

_____ 3.29. In Cameron Park, as in all colonias along the Rio Grande, the least important need is housing. (134)

C. **Multiple-Choice Questions on Text Material** (with textbook page numbers)

_____ 3.30. The authors of *Practicing Texas Politics* use the term grassroots to describe (90)

    a. the national government.
    b. regional governments.
    c. state governments.
    d. governments of cities, counties, and special districts.

_____ 3.31. Municipalities in Texas are classified as home-rule cities and (92)

    a. statutory-law cities.
    b. constitutional-law cities.
    c. general-law cities.
    d. local-option cities.

_____ 3.32. In a home-rule city, a citizen-drafted measure may be initiated by a certain number of qualified voters; and, if approved in a referendum vote, it will become a local law known as a(n) (92)

    a. ordinance.
    b. statute.
    c. amendment.
    d. proposition.

_____ 3.33. A mayor with power to appoint and remove department heads, to prepare and execute a budget, and to veto actions of the city's principal
policymaking body would be serving in a city with a (93)

    a.   strong mayor-council form of government.
    b.   weak mayor-council form of government.
    c.   council-manager form of government.
    d.   commission form of government.

_____ 3.34. Once a policy is made, the city manager's office directs an appropriate
department to (96)

    a.   endorse it.
    b.   implement it.
    c.   adjudicate it.
    d.   deliberate it.

_____ 3.35. When each voter in a municipal election casts a single vote for a council candidate seeking to represent the part of the city where the voter
lives, that city has been divided into (98)

    a.   single-member districts.
    b.   flotorial districts.
    c.   nonpartisan districts.
    d.   home-rule districts.

_____ 3.36. Where the place system is used for electing members of the city council, a voter's maximum authorized voting activity involves voting for
(99)

    a.   a single candidate residing in the voter's district.
    b.   all candidates on the ballot.
    c.   all candidates nominated by the voter's party.
    d.   one candidate for each numerically designated place.

_____ 3.37. Use of single-member districts for electing city council members in
major cities tends to make municipal government more responsive to
the residents of (100)

    a.   adjoining suburbs.
    b.   nearby colonias.
    c.   the central city.
    d.   affluent neighborhoods.

3.38.   Among Texas's 10 largest municipalities, the only one that does not have zoning power is (100)

   a.   Dallas.
   b.   El Paso.
   c.   Houston.
   d.   San Antonio.

3.39.   Texas municipalities are authorized to levy (101)

   a.   a personal income tax.
   b.   a tax on corporate income.
   c.   a general property tax.
   d.   a tariff on foreign-manufactured goods.

3.40.   A fee based on the gross receipts of public utilities such as telephone companies is called (101)

   a.   a user fee.
   b.   an excise fee.
   c.   a communication fee.
   d.   a franchise fee.

3.41.   A municipality would be most likely to issue revenue bonds to raise money for (102)

   a.   paying salaries to police officers.
   b.   constructing a fire station.
   c.   constructing a money-making power plant for a city-operated electric utility.
   d.   renting office space for city welfare personnel.

3.42.   Texas cities may issue bonds, provided they assess taxes and collect sufficient revenue to pay the interest and retire the principal without (102)

   a.   alienating citizens.
   b.   offending the business community.
   c.   creating a budget surplus.
   d.   exceeding legal tax limits.

3.43.   Tax reinvestment zones (TRZs) are established by cities in order to (103)

   a.   suppress crime.
   b.   divert surplus revenue.
   c.   equalize the tax burden among consumers.
   d.   attract new businesses to blighted areas.

_____ 3.44. According to the Texas Constitution, the county is (103)

    a. a creature of the federal government.
    b. a sovereign, independent political entity.
    c. a private corporation.
    d. an administrative arm of the state.

_____ 3.45. Presiding at meetings of the county commissioners court is the county (104)

    a. sheriff.
    b. judge.
    c. attorney.
    d. clerk.

_____ 3.46. Each Texas county is divided into four county commissioner (104)

    a. wards.
    b. parishes.
    c. precincts.
    d. stakes.

_____ 3.47. The county tax assessor-collector (108)

    a. appraises all real estate in the county for taxation by all taxing authorities in the county.
    b. collects license fees for motor vehicles.
    c. appraises all real estate in the county for taxation by the county government only.
    d. collects a state poll tax.

_____ 3.48. Although prescribed by the Texas Constitution, most counties do not fill the elective office of county (109)

    a. scalper.
    b. hunter.
    c. ranger.
    d. surveyor.

_____ 3.49. In most of Texas's rural counties, the budget item requiring the largest expenditures is that for (110)

    a. roads and bridges.
    b. parks and recreation.
    c. welfare.
    d. law enforcement.

3.50. Subject to voter approval, the board for a Texas junior or community college district (113)

    a.   adopts textbooks.
    b.   sets property tax rates.
    c.   adopts an annual budget.
    d.   issues bonds.

3.51. Among Texas's noneducation special districts, the largest number are classified as (115)

    a.   hospital districts.
    b.   soil and water conservation districts.
    c.   housing authorities.
    d.   water or utility districts.

3.52. Ringing Texas's large cities are rapidly growing (116)

    a.   farming operations.
    b.   ranching operations.
    c.   suburban communities.
    d.   central cities.

3.53. Membership in a council of governments (COG) is (117)

    a.   voluntary for all units of local government.
    b.   mandatory for cities but voluntary for special districts.
    c.   mandatory for counties but voluntary for cities.
    d.   mandatory for all units of local government within each county that is associated with a COG.

3.54 If a home-rule city does not provide water and sewer services to an annexed area, the area's residents can petition a state district court for (118)

    a.   municipal compensation.
    b.   county-funded services.
    c.   special district status.
    d.   deannexation.

3.55. To protect property owners, before an unwanted municipal annexation can occur, the annexing Texas city must wait for a period of (118)

    a.   1 year.
    b.   3 years.
    c.   6 years.
    d.   10 years.

D. **Multiple-Choice Questions on Readings** (with textbook page numbers)

_____ 3.56. Prior to being elected to public office, Laura Miller was employed as a (122)

    a. school teacher.
    b. lawyer.
    c. emergency-room physician.
    d. news-weekly reporter.

_____ 3.57. In the January 2002, in the first round of the electoral contest for the office of mayor of Dallas, Laura Miller finished (124)

    a. first with 100 percent of the vote.
    b. first with 55 percent of the vote.
    c. first with 48.8 percent of the vote.
    d. second with 39 percent of the vote.

_____ 3.58. Among controversial issues leading to term limits for members of San Antonio's city council was a collective bargaining agreement with the city's (126)

    a. Chamber of Commerce.
    b. tourist guides.
    c. city council.
    d. Police Officers Association.

_____ 3.59. Within three months after taking office, San Antonio's city council members are (127)

    a. required to pass a written examination composed of questions covering the city's charter and ordinances.
    b. required to pass a rigorous physical examination.
    c. presented with a proposed consolidated annual budget for the city.
    d. forced to begin campaigning for reelection.

_____ 3.60. The community center in Cameron Park was built with the help of the Colonias Program of (133)

    a. the University of Texas—Brownsville.
    b. St. Mary's University.
    c. Baylor University.
    d. Texas A&M University.

_____ 3.61. The Community Development Corporation of Brownsville and the Rio Grande Valley Multibank have helped Cameron Park residents obtain (134)

    a. loans for purchase of lottery tickets.

    b. transportation, taking them to agricultural jobs in California and Michigan.

    c. grants for graduate school education.

    d. home mortgages.

E. Completion Questions on Text Material (with textbook page numbers)

3.62. Compared to general-law cities, home-rule cities in Texas have greater flexibility in determining the form and structure of municipal _____. (92)

3.63. The recall provision of Austin's charter provides for removal of elected officials through a popular _____. (92)

3.64. Under the weak mayor-council form of government, the _____ exercises limited administrative powers. (93)

3.65. Under the council-manager system, the city _____ is responsible for budget coordination. (96)

3.66. A new era in municipal administration began in 1913 when Amarillo and Terrel adopted the _____ form of government. (96)

3.67. Establishing long-standing relationships between a city manager and city council members is sometimes hampered by the fact that some city councils are subject to term _____. (98)

3.68. In theory, council-manager systems attempt to separate policymaking and _____. (98)

3.69. All elected officials for Texas municipalities are elected in state-mandated _____ elections. (98)

3.70. All members of city councils for Dallas, San Antonio, Fort Worth, and El Paso are elected from _____ districts. (98-99)

3.71. Texas cities may charge a _____ fee based on the gross receipts of public utilities operating within their jurisdictions. (101)

3.72. When faced with a budget problem, one option for a municipal government would be to impose hiring and wage _____ on city employees. (103)

3.73. In Texas, county commissioners are elected for a term of _____ years. (104)

3.74. Maintaining a Texas county's vital statistics is the responsibility of the county _____. (108)

3.75. Assessing business and residential property for tax purposes within each Texas county is the function of a countywide tax _____ district. (108)

3.76. The _____ function involves checking records and account books of all county officials who handle county funds. (109)

3.77. Farm and ranch land in Texas is taxed on the basis of _____ rather than market value. (109)

3.78. County governments are authorized to keep half of the fees collected for issuing certificates of _____ for motor vehicles. (110)

3.79. County expenditures for welfare and mental health programs are examples of spending that is dictated by the _____, not by the county. (111)

3.80. School districts and _____ special districts are the two basic categories of special district governments. (112)

3.81. Among the powers conferred on school boards by the Texas Legislature is the power to provide for the construction and _____ of school buildings. (112)

3.82. A recent study shows that community colleges stimulate the local _____. (114)

3.83. The phrase "review and comment" refers to a COG's evaluation function concerning _____ proposals submitted by member governments. (117)

3.84. Consolidation of local government units within an urban area under one umbrella is called _____ government. (118)

F.   Completion Questions on Readings (with textbook page numbers)

3.85. In announcing her candidacy for the office of mayor of Dallas, Laura Miller told supporters that she would focus on "_____ things" like roads, parks, swimming pools, and safer neighborhoods. (123)

3.86. In her campaign for mayor of Dallas, Laura Miller received help from _____ groups after she promised to raise their pay. (124)

3.87. Alexander E. Briseno compares service on San Antonio's city council to serving on the board of directors of a _____ 1000 company. (127)

3.88. Alexander E. Briseno concludes that San Antonio's "_____" term limits are frequently counterproductive. (130)

3.89. Cameron Park's _____ serve as an important means for community activists to communicate information to residents. (133)

3.90. According to Cecilia Balli, the ultimate test of how far Cameron Park has progressed will be whether the City of Brownsville will _____ it. (134)

G. Essay Questions (with textbook page numbers)

1. Describe the four basic forms of municipal government operating in Texas. (92-98)
2. Identify the two basic types of municipal election systems and comment on their use in selected Texas cities. (98-100)
3. Describe the principal means whereby revenue is obtained to support the programs of Texas's cities, and note innovative ways of raising revenue for economic development. (100-103)
4. Identify four Texas county officials (not including the county commissioners and county judge), and describe their principal powers and functions. (108-109)
5. Describe the principal sources of revenue for financing the governments of Texas's counties. (109-110)
6. Write an essay entitled "The Importance of Noneducation Special Districts in Texas." Explain why these districts must be classified as units of government and identify some of their characteristics. (115)
7. Write an essay on "Special Problems of Government in Texas's Metropolitan Areas." In your essay, identify some of the problems, describe steps taken to cope with these problems, and suggest measures that you recommend for solving these problems in the future. (116-118)
8. Based on How Do We Compare data provided at the top of page 91 in this chapter, identify some differences and similarities with regard to numbers of cities and counties in the 12 states. Do these data appear to be related to data for area and population provided in How Do We Compare tables on pages 8 and 16 in Chapter 1?

III. Applying Your Knowledge

A. Outside Readings and Cartoons

1. From the endnotes for this chapter or from the updated bibliography of selected sources accessible through the Houghton Mifflin Political Science home page (politicalscience.college.hmco.com), choose a magazine or journal article and write a summary of it.

2. From the endnotes or selected sources for this chapter or from the updated bibliography of selected sources accessible through the Houghton Mifflin Political Science home page (politicalscience.college.hmco.com), choose a book and write a summary of one of its chapters.
3. In a Texas newspaper, find an editorial that relates to municipal, county, or special-district government. Summarize that editorial, and explain why you agree or disagree with the writer's point of view.
4. Find a newspaper article concerning municipal, county, or special-district government in Texas. Summarize the article, and describe what you do and/or do not like about this piece of reporting.
5. Interpret one of this chapter's cartoons (or another cartoon concerning local government), and explain why you agree or disagree with the cartoonist's viewpoint.
6. Explore two or more of the web sites listed among sources for this chapter. Then select one site and write a brief note outlining how its information contributes to your understanding of local governments in Texas.

B.   Internet Research Project

Objectives

1. To enhance student understanding of the functions of the county judge.
2. To enhance student understanding of the functions of the commissioners court.
3. To introduce students to the difference between query-driven research requests and subject-driven research requests on the Internet.

URL. http://www.co.bexar.tx.us

Description of the Site. Bexar County, like many Texas counties, has developed its own web site. The site includes extensive information about Bexar County and county governmental functions—from employment opportunities with the county to the minutes of county commissioners' weekly meetings to a history of Bexar County courthouses. Further, all of this information has been indexed on the site. After the "Search" page, a researcher can type in a name or phrase. The search can be customized by clicking on the "Options" key and identifying proximity of words to each other, word forms, and the most important characteristics of the search. An index of all documents on the site that contain the name or phrase is displayed on the screen. The researcher can then click on the title to view the entire document.

Use of Information. Using the web site for Bexar County (http://www.co.bexar.tx.us), you will conduct research on the county judge and the commissioners court.

1. Once you are on Bexar County's home page, type "county judge" in the query box to the right of "Search." Then click on "go" to reach "county judge" in hypertext. Click here to reach the page for the county judge, whose name is

   _____.

2. Click on the "Biosketch" button to find answers to the following questions:
   a. When was the judge last elected? _____
   b. What are some of the other offices, if any, that the judge has held?
      (1) _____
      (2) _____
      (3) _____
      (4) _____
   c. What are the titles of books, if any, authored by the judge?
      (1) _____
      (2) _____

3. Click on the button for FAQs (frequently asked questions) to identify:
   a. Four responsibilities of the county judge:
      (1) _____
      (2) _____
      (3) _____
      (4) _____
   b. Four responsibilities of the commissioners court:
      (1) _____
      (2) _____
      (3) _____
      (4) _____
   c. Information concerning regular meetings of the commissioners court.
      (1) day: _____
      (2) time: _____
      (3) place: _____

4. Click on the "Speeches" button. Then click on the hypertext for the title of a speech. After reading the speech,
   a. list four Bexar County problems or issues identified by the judge:
      (1) _____
      (2) _____
      (3) _____
      (4) _____

    b.   list four recent acts of the judge that are mentioned:

       (1) _____

       (2) _____

       (3) _____

       (4) _____

Internet Research Tip. In conducting research on the Internet, you will need to select a search service or engine. Search services are like card catalogs in libraries. They are used to index the contents of web sites.

Some services use query-driven searches in which the researcher enters a word or phrase, and all web sites that use that word or phrase are identified by hyperlinks. This type of search is effective in searching for a specific phrase if an organization's title is known. Many services even rate identified web sites on how responsive they are to the request. If you are having trouble drafting your query, check under the "Help" section of the search engine. This section often provides tips on how to search for the information you need. In the exercise above, you were asked to conduct a query-driven search.

Other services use subject-driven searches. The search service prepares a directory. Web sites are organized by the identified categories. In conducting a subject-driven search, you will need to identify the general category to be investigated. Each general category will be a hyperlink to more specific subcategories. Through these subcategories you will be able to reach relevant web sites. This type of search is most effective for locating the major sites for a particular subject. Often both types of searches should be used to assure that a thorough inquiry has been made for available Internet sources.

Answers

True-False: Text	Multiple-Choice: Text	Completion: Text
3.1. F	3.30. d	3.62. government
3.2. F	3.31. c	3.63. vote
3.3. T	3.32. a	3.64. mayor
3.4. F	3.33. a	3.65. manager
3.5. F	3.34. b	3.66. council-manager
3.6. F	3.35. a	3.67. limits
3.7. T	3.36. d	3.68. administration
3.8. T	3.37. c	3.69. nonpartisan
3.9. F	3.38. c	3.70. single-member
3.10. T	3.39. c	3.71. franchise
3.11. F	3.40. d	3.72. freezes
3.12. T	3.41. c	3.73. four
3.13. T	3.42. d	3.74. clerk
3.14. T	3.43. d	3.75. appraisal
3.15. F	3.44. d	3.76. auditing
3.16. T	3.45. b	3.77. productivity
3.17. T	3.46. c	3.78. title
3.18. T	3.47. b	3.79. state
3.19. T	3.48. d	3.80. noneducation
3.20. F	3.49. a	3.81. maintenance
3.21. F	3.50. d	3.82. transit
3.22. T	3.51. d	3.83. grant
3.23. T	3.52. c	3.84. metro
	3.53. a	
	3.54. d	

True-False: Readings

3.55. b

	Completion: Readings
3.24. T	3.85. little
3.25. T	3.86. police
3.26. T	3.87. *Fortune*
3.27. F	3.88. extreme
3.28. T	3.89. churches
3.29. F	3.90. annex

Multiple-Choice: Readings

3.56. d
3.57. c
3.58. d
3.59. c
3.60. d
3.61. d

CHAPTER FOUR

The Politics of Elections and Parties

I. *Preparing to Study*

A. Performance Objectives

After studying and reviewing the text and readings in this chapter, you will be able to:

1. Identify important obstacles to voting that have been removed in the course of democratizing the ballot in Texas since the Civil War.
2. List legal qualifications for voting in Texas.
3. Describe the process of registering to vote in Texas.
4. Explain how and when Texas voters may vote early, "in person" and "by mail."
5. Outline important details concerning the administration of direct primaries and general elections in Texas.
6. Identify and describe the temporary and permanent organizational structures of Texas's Democratic and Republican parties.
7. Describe important ideological differences between liberalism and conservatism.
8. Outline Texas political history from the 1840s through 2002.
9. Describe the recent rise of the Texas Republican Party and the decline of the Texas Democratic Party.
10. Identify "third parties" whose candidates have been listed on Texas ballots, and comment on their ideologies and their influence on the outcome of elections.
11. Compare and contrast recent political gains of African Americans and Latinos in Texas.
12. Discuss recent advances by women in Texas politics.
13. Discuss the conduct of recent Texas political campaigns, and present your ideas regarding the issues of campaign reform and campaign finance.

B. **Overview of the Text** (pp. 136–181)

Representative democracy is based on political participation by the people. In recent years, however, there has been a decline of participation in Texas.

Voting (pp. 136–144). Universal suffrage was slow in coming to Texas. After the Civil War, the Fourteenth and Fifteenth Amendments to the U.S. Constitution were supposed to prevent denial of voting because of race. Nevertheless, Ku Klux Klan terrorism, literacy tests, grandfather clauses, poll taxes, white primaries, racial gerrymandering, and diluting minority votes have been obstacles. Federal courts and the U.S. Congress have been instrumental in removing most obstacles. Today, almost any Texas resident 18 years of age or older can register and vote in general and special elections and in party primaries.

Electoral Politics (pp. 144–152). In Texas, direct primaries are used to nominate Democratic and Republican candidates. Because nomination of a candidate requires an absolute majority vote, the first primary is held on the first Tuesday in March, and (as needed) a second or runoff primary is conducted on the first Tuesday in April. Primaries are financed by a combination of filing fees and state funding.

As in other parts of the country, general elections are held in Texas on the first Tuesday following the first Monday in November of even-numbered years. Special elections to fill vacancies in U.S. congressional and state legislative offices, to approve proposed state constitutional amendments, and, occasionally, to elect certain local government officials are held as needed. The candidate receiving the most votes (a plurality) is the winner in a general election contest. If no candidate receives an absolute majority in a special election, a runoff between the top two candidates is required. The voting precinct is the basic geographic area for conducting elections. State laws concerning electoral matters are compiled in the Texas Election Code.

Party Structure (pp. 152–158). Texas's Democratic and Republican parties are similar in structure. They have temporary and permanent organizations. Primaries and conventions are temporary, but county, district, and state executive committees are parts of each party's permanent organization. Precinct conventions are held on the day of the first primary. The purpose of a precinct convention is to name delegates who will attend a county convention (or a senatorial district convention in a heavily populated county in which two or more state senators are elected). County and district conventions are held on the second Saturday after the first primary. One of the purposes of these conventions is to elect delegates to attend a party's state convention, which is held in June of each even-numbered year.

In Texas, each political party's permanent organizational structure is headed by a state executive committee composed of 31 men, 31 women, a chair, and a vice chair. At the bottom of each state structure, a party can have 254 county executive committees. A county executive committee is composed of all the voting-precinct chairs in the county plus the county chair. These party officials are elected in the party primaries that are used for nominating candidates for public offices. A district executive committee consists of all county executive committee chairs in a district (such as a state senatorial district or a U.S. congressional district). If a district consists of only one county or part of a county, the precinct chairs within that district make up the district executive committee.

Political Democracy (pp. 158–166). Since the 1930s, the terms liberal and conservative have had more meaning for many Texas voters than Democratic and Republican party labels. Conservative doctrine calls for minimum social services and little government intervention in economic affairs; liberal doctrine supports government involvement to promote a more equal distribution of wealth and more extensive delivery of social services.

When Texas was an independent republic, Texans were divided into pro (Sam) Houston and anti-Houston groups. Before the Civil War, the principal political groups were the Jackson Democrats and the Calhoun Democrats. The Republican Party dominated the state during the Reconstruction era following the war. With the end of the E. J. Davis administration, the Democratic Party was dominant for more than a century; but Texas Democrats were divided into liberal and conservative factions. In 1961, a special election gave Republican John Tower a seat in the U.S. Senate. This event marked the beginning of four decades of GOP growth and the decline of the Democratic Party. In 2003, Texas Republicans had majorities in both houses of the legislature and held all statewide elective offices.

Political Parties (pp. 166–170) By the 1990s, Texas had become a two-party state. In addition to the Republican and Democratic parties, a few "third parties" have nominated some candidates for statewide office and placed their presidential candidates on the general election ballot. In 2002 the most active third parties in Texas were the Libertarian Party, the Green Party, and the Reform Party.

Racial/Ethnic Politics (pp. 170–173). Minority voters and candidates, especially Latinos, are playing a larger role in Texas elections. Democrat Dan Morales won two terms as the state's attorney general in the 1999s, and Tony Sanchez became the Democratic Party's first gubernatorial candidate in 2002. Both George W. Bush and Rick Perry courted Latino voters by speaking Spanish and appointing Latinos to high state offices. Traditionally, most African-American Texans and a large majority of Latinos have supported Democratic candidates. Over the last two decades, African-American and Latino representation has increased in the Texas Legislature.

Women in Politics (pp. 173–174). After the impeachment and removal of Governor Jim (Pa) Ferguson, his wife, Miriam A. (Ma) Ferguson was elected to two nonconsecutive, two-year terms (1925-1926 and 1933-1935) as governor. It was not until the 1990s, however, that Ann Richards served a four-year term as governor, Kaye Bailey Hutchison began to serve in the U.S. Senate, and an impressive number of Texas women began to win other high offices. In recent years, several of the state's cities (including Houston, Dallas, El Paso, San Antonio, and Waco) have elected women as mayors.

Political Campaigns (pp. 175–180). Campaigning by candidates in Texas no longer emphasizes speeches delivered from courthouse steps or the rear platform of a train. E-mail, web sites, television, opinion polls, and professional campaign personnel have been added to the more traditional means of campaigning; and the cost of running for office has escalated. Nevertheless, candidates tend to conduct mud-slinging campaigns that often fail to deal with important public policy issues. Most of what citizens learn about office-seekers is the result of viewing their short, expensive, and frequently negative TV commercials. Efforts to reform the electoral process focus on eliminating negative campaigning, increasing free media access for candidates, and imposing limits on campaign contributions and spending. Meanwhile, voter participation is declining.

Looking Ahead (p. 180–181). The U.S. Supreme Court has ruled that Americans have the right to contribute money to candidates and to spend money on their own campaigns. Because of the high cost of running for office and fear of undue influence by PACs, some people have called for public financing of election campaigns. At this point, however, most Texans are not prepared to support reforms that would limit the political influence of wealthy individuals and powerful interest groups.

C. Key Terms (with textbook page numbers)

universal suffrage (136)
literacy tests (136)
grandfather clause (137)
Gwinn v. *United States* (137)
poll tax (137)
Harper v. *Virginia State Board of*
   Elections (137)
white primary (137)
Smith v. *Allwright* (138)
racial gerrymandering (138)
Shaw v. *Reno* (138)

at-large majority district (138)
motor voter law (138)
Fifteenth Amendment (139)
Nineteenth Amendment (139)
Twenty-Fourth Amendment (139)
Twenty-Sixth Amendment (139)
Texas Election Code (139)
voter registration (140)
elections administrator (140)
early voting (143)
direct primary (144)

D. Overview of the Readings (pp. 185–192)

4.1. "Elephant Wars: The Christian Right Flexes Its Muscle At the Republican Convention" by Jake Bernstein (pp. 185–189)

At the Texas Republican state convention in 2002, a platform was adopted that included many controversial planks. Included were provisions for "American English" as the Lone Star State's official language, deportation of aliens without required ID cards, repeal of hate crimes legislation, termination of bilingual education programs, prosecution of women who get abortions, repeal of the minimum wage law, adoption of a constitutional amendment incorporating Right-to-Work legislation, evicting the United Nations from the United States and ending U.S. membership, regaining the Panama Canal, and abolishing several agencies of the U.S. government. To ensure support of the platform, some delegates fought for a version of Rule 43 penalizing politicians condemned as RINOs (Republican in Name Only). If adopted, it would have withheld party funding for candidates who did not take a stand on each plank.

4.2. "Swept Away" by Paul Burka (pp. 189–192)

Paul Burka, the senior executive editor of *Texas Monthly*, explains that the Democratic Party's strategy for winning Texas's 2002 electoral contests failed because Democrats (1) alienated white voters, (2) overestimated Hispanic solidarity, (3) overestimated Hispanic turnout, and (4) counted on ticket splitters. Burka concludes that Texas has become "an overwhelmingly Republican state," and he believes that the crushing GOP victory "calls into question whether the Democratic party has any near-term future in Texas." Meanwhile, he says Democrats can wait for the GOP to "make a mistake"—but the large number of Republicans suggests "even that might not be enough."

II.   *Testing Your Knowledge*

A.   True-False Questions on Text Material (with textbook page numbers)

_____ 4.1. The 14th and 15th Amendments to the U.S. Constitution were added after the Civil War. (136)

_____ 4.2. The Twenty-fourth Amendment to the U.S. Constitution eliminated the poll tax as a prerequisite for voting in national elections. (137)

_____ 4.3. In Texas, voter registration requires the personal appearance of a prospective voter in the office of the county voting registrar. (138)

_____ 4.4. Under Texas law, a felony conviction results in permanent disqualification from voting. (140)

_____ 4.5. In Texas elections, the turnout rate for African Americans has been substantially below that for Anglos. (143)

_____ 4.6. Under Texas law, early voting is not allowed in party primaries or general elections. (143)

_____ 4.7. In the Texas primary system, a Democratic contestant who receives the most votes in the first primary always becomes the Democratic Party's nominee. (144)

_____ 4.8. A Texas voter makes a party pledge at the time of voting in a primary. (146)

_____ 4.9. Prospective candidates desiring to have their names placed on the primary ballot for county or precinct office must file with the county chair of their party. (147)

_____ 4.10. Payment of a filing fee is the only way that a candidate may obtain a place on a Texas primary ballot. (147)

_____ 4.11. Part of the expense of conducting Texas primaries is paid by the state. (147)

_____ 4.12. Each county in Texas has a county election commission that designates polling places used in general elections. (149)

_____ 4.13. Under an "English only" law, ballots used in Texas primaries and elections must be printed only in English. (152)

_____ 4.14. In Texas, temporary organizations of political parties last for periods of a few hours or one or two days. (154)

_____ 4.15. The lowest level of temporary party organization is the precinct convention. (154)

_____ 4.16 While running for governor of Texas in 1998, George W. Bush has used the phrase "compassionate conservatism" to identify his political philosophy. (159)

_____ 4.17. Today's political liberals favor government regulation so that wealth may be more equitably distributed. (159)

_____ 4.18. Political realignment involves a shift in party affiliation. (166)

_____ 4.19 The Permian Basin area of West Texas has been a stronghold of the Democratic Party since 1980. (166)

_____ 4.20 The term "third party" is commonly used to describe either the Republican Party or the Democratic Party. (158)

_____ 4.21. According to Ruben Bonilla, the Raza Unida Party did not survive because of the maturity of the Republican Party to accept African Americans. (171)

_____ 4.22. Dan Morales, a Democrat, was elected twice to the office of attorney general. (171)

_____ 4.23. Difficulty in raising money for campaign expenses is the chief reason fewer women than men run for elective public office. (174)

_____ 4.24. W. Lee "Pappy O'Daniel was a TV host for General Motors and ran unsuccessfully for governor in 1938. (175)

_____ 4.25. Usually, it is the candidate who is behind in the polls who wants to debate his or her opponent. (176)

_____ 4.26. Neither Rick Perry nor Tony Sanchez used negative TV ads in their gubernatorial election campaigns in 2002. (177)

B. **True-False Questions on Readings** (with textbook page numbers)

_____ 4.27. The Texas Republican Party platform of 2002 included a plank to repeal the state's minimum wage law. (185)

_____ 4.28. Republicans in Name Only (RINOs) is a term used by some Texas Republicans to describe those GOP politicians who do not support fully their party's platform. (186)

_____ 4.29. Paul Burka states that the Democratic Party's "turn out the minority vote" strategy in 2002 alienated the white vote. (190)

_____ 4.30. Paul Burka states that Democratic Party strategy in 2002 underestimated Hispanic solidarity. (190)

C. **Multiple-Choice Questions on Text Material** (with textbook page numbers)

_____ 4.31. Universal suffrage did not become a reality in Texas until (136)

    a. the mid-1960s.
    b. the end of World War II in 1945.
    c. the end of World War I in 1918.
    d. the end of the Civil War in 1865.

_____ 4.32. The U.S. Supreme Court's decision in *Smith* v. *Allwright* (1944) invalidated Texas's (137-138)

    a. poll tax as a prerequisite for voting.
    b. poll tax as the Lone Star State's principal means of raising revenue.
    c. anti-Ku Klux Klan legislation.
    d. white primary.

_____ 4.33. Among qualifications for voting in Texas is the requirement that one must be (139)

    a. a native-born citizen of the United States.
    b. at least 18 years of age on or before Election Day.
    c. a resident of the state, county, and election precinct at least 60 days immediately preceding Election Day.
    d. a registered voter for at least one day immediately preceding Election Day.

4.34. A Texas voter registration certificate is issued between November 1 and 15 of (140)

a. each presidential election year.
b. each year.
c. each gubernatorial election year.
d. each odd-numbered year.

4.35. Democratization of the ballot has been largely the result of pressure from the (141)

a. federal government.
b. state governments.
c. county governments.
d. municipal governments.

4.36. Of all the socioeconomic influences on voting, the strongest by far is that of (142)

a. education.
b. race.
c. age.
d. sex.

4.37. Texas's 17-day early voting period applies to (143)

a. runoff primaries only.
b. first primaries only.
c. general elections only.
d. all first primaries and general elections.

4.38. In Texas, polling places for early voting are generally open on weekdays (143)

a. during general business hours of the official conducting the election.
b. from 8 a.m. to 11:30 a.m.
c. from 1 p.m. to 5 p.m.
d. from 9 a.m. to 4 p.m.

4.39. Except for the purpose of nominating presidential and vice presidential candidates and some local officials, voters in every state nominate candidates for other public offices through use of some form of (144)

a. convention system.
b. caucus system.
c. appointment system.
d. direct primary system.

_____ 4.40. Declaration of party affiliation when registering or voting is required in states using the (144)

    a. open primary system.
    b. indirect primary system.
    c. closed primary system.
    d. blanket primary system.

_____ 4.41. Primaries are administered in most states by (146)

    a. agents of the federal government.
    b. sponsoring political parties.
    c. agents of state governments who are employed by a state attorney general or a secretary of state.
    d. a combination of government officials at the local, state, and national levels.

_____ 4.42. First primaries for Texas Democrats and Republicans are conducted on the (146)

    a. first Saturday in January in odd-numbered years.
    b. first Tuesday in March in even-numbered years.
    c. first Saturday in May in odd-numbered years.
    d. fourth Saturday in June in even-numbered years.

_____ 4.43. In Texas, general elections for state, district, and county officials are held in (148)

    a. November of even-numbered years.
    b. March of odd-numbered years.
    c. April of even-numbered years.
    d. May of odd-numbered years.

_____ 4.44. In Texas, general elections for selecting the governor and other state-wide officers serving four-year terms have been scheduled to (148)

    a. coincide with elections to fill municipal offices.
    b. coincide with elections to fill special-district offices.
    c. avoid the influence of presidential elections.
    d. avoid the influence of congressional elections.

_____ 4.45. The basic unit for conducting national, state, district, and county elections in Texas is the voting (149)

    a. district.
    b. area.
    c. region.
    d. precinct.

_____ 4.46. Voting-precinct clerks who help conduct Texas's general and special elections must be selected from different (149)

      a. ethnic groups.
      b. political parties.
      c. racial groups.
      d. geographic areas.

_____ 4.47. In Texas, both Spanish and English registration and election materials are used in (152)

      a. South Texas counties only.
      b. metropolitan areas only.
      c. counties with Latino population majorities only.
      d. all counties.

_____ 4.48. One major function of a Texas party's state convention is to (154)

      a. adopt a party platform.
      b. nominate the party's candidate for the office of governor.
      c. issue voting directives for the party's delegation to the U.S. House of Representatives.
      d. nominate the party's candidate for the office of secretary of state.

_____ 4.49. The Texas Republican Party selects delegates to the national GOP convention based on the results of (156)

      a. the presidential preference primary.
      b. casting lots.
      c. written examinations for prospective delegates.
      d. appointments made by the state executive committee.

_____ 4.50. One man and one woman from each of Texas's state senatorial districts, along with a chair and a vice chair, compose a party's (157)

      a. senatorial committee.
      b. local government committee.
      c. state executive committee.
      d. delegation to the national presidential convention.

_____ 4.51. Internal feuding within a political party is termed (158)

      a. radicalism.
      b. factionalism.
      c. feudalism.
      d. humanism.

4.52. Texas conservatives are more likely than liberals to oppose (159)

    a. church involvement in secular politics.
    b. mandatory prayer in public schools.
    c. government subsidies for religious institutions.
    d. government assistance to poor families.

4.53. The ideological position that advocates fiscal conservatism but allows for a limited government role in solving social problems reflects (159)

    a. the socialist view.
    b. the neoliberal view.
    c. the neoconservative view.
    d. the communist view.

4.54. In the gubernatorial election of 1998, Republican candidate George W. Bush's share of the vote was almost (163)

    a. 70 percent.
    b. 59 percent.
    c. 49 percent.
    d. 30 percent.

4.55. From 1994 to 2002, the Republican primary vote was larger than the Democratic primary vote in (167)

    a. gubernatorial election years only.
    b. presidential election years only.
    c. both gubernatorial and presidential election years.
    d. neither gubernatorial nor presidential election years.

4.56. A "yellow dog Democrat" is a person who (168)

    a. is intensely loyal to the Democratic Party and its candidates.
    b. leaves the Democratic Party and joins the GOP.
    c. participates in Democratic primaries but votes for Republican candidates in general elections.
    d. identifies with the Democratic Party but is dedicated to the cause of People for the Ethical Treatment of Animals.

4.57. The Texas Libertarian Party advocates (169)

    a. minimizing the performance of government at all levels.
    b. minimizing individual freedom.
    c. minimizing individual rights.
    d. regulating the sale and use of drugs.

4.58. Texas's Green Party is known for its (169)

   a. opposition to campaign finance reform.
   b. advocacy of lower taxes on the wealthy.
   c. support of environmental protection policies.
   d. defense of political influence by corporate wealth and power.

4.59. Most Texans learn about candidates for public office through (176)

   a. radio news broadcasts.
   b. television commercials.
   c. newspaper editorials.
   d. telephone calls.

4.60. Texas law requires disclosure of information relating to (180)

   a. political ideology of professors at state universities.
   b. amounts of election campaign contributions and expenditures.
   c. social activities of state employees.
   d. ethics indoctrination for officeholders and candidates for public office.

D. Multiple-Choice Questions on Readings (with textbook page numbers)

4.61. Included in the Texas Republican Party's 2002 platform was a plank endorsing (185)

   a. racial segregation in public schools.
   b. ethnic segregation in public schools.
   c. extended coverage of the state's labor force by workers' compensation laws.
   d. reasonable use of racial profiling by law enforcement officers.

4.62. At the Texas Republican Party's 2002 convention, an unsuccessful effort was made to adopt a version of Rule 43 that would have withheld party funding from GOP candidates who failed to declare that they approved, disapproved or were undecided about (188)

   a. President George W. Bush's policies concerning Iraq.
   b. each plank in the Texas GOP's platform.
   c. redistricting for U.S. representatives elected in Texas.
   d. free trade with all Latin American countries.

_____ 4.63. Paul Burka states that the most startling development in Texas's 2002 election was (191)

    a. the inability of gubernatorial candidate Tony Sanchez to raise campaign funds.

    b. the large percentage of African Americans who supported GOP candidates.

    c. the disappearance of ticket splitters.

    d. the popularity of John Sharp with Republican voters.

_____ 4.64. Paul Burka is of the opinion that the Texas Republican Party's victory in 2002 calls into question whether the Democratic Party has any (191)

    a. hope of winning either state or local offices in 2006.

    b. chance of gubernatorial victories in the twenty-first century.

    c. near-term future in the state.

    d. hope of retaining the support of minority voters.

E.   **Completion Questions on Text Material** (with textbook page numbers)

4.65. The _____ primary was devised and used in Texas to prevent African Americans and some Latinos from voting in the Democratic primary. (137)

4.66. Voter _____ is intended to determine in advance whether prospective voters meet all of the qualifications prescribed by law. (140)

4.67. In a local election at the city or school-district level in Texas, a _____ of 20 percent is considered relatively high. (141)

4.68. _____ voting in Texas is allowed during the 17-day period preceding a first primary or general election. (143)

4.69. At the top of each ballot used in a Texas primary is printed a statement that the voter will be "ineligible to vote or participate in another political party's primary election or _____ during the voting year." (146)

4.70. Under Texas law, run-off primaries are held on the first Tuesday in _____. (146)

4.71. One method of voting in Texas involves use of the direct-record electronic (or _____) system. (150)

4.72. Within the limits of Texas law, the voting system used in a county is determined by the county _____ court. (150)

4.73. When voting, Texans may take voting guides and other printed materials into a voting _____. (152)

4.74. Conventions constitute components of the _____ party organization for each major political party in Texas. (154)

4.75. In Texas, the state executive committee constitutes the highest _____ party organization for each major political party. (157)

4.76. Conservative doctrine advocates an economic system that is largely untouched by _____. (159)

4.77. Straight-ticket voting has been the practice of Texas's "yellow _____ Democrats." (168)

4.78. In 1996, Ross Perot launched a new political party named the _____ Party. (168)

4.79. The Raza Unida Party was founded in 1969 by José Angel Gutiérrez of _____ City and others. (171)

4.80. In a 1990 contest for a seat on the Texas Court of Criminal Appeals, the racial classification of both the Democratic candidate (Morris Overstreet) and the Republican candidate (Louis Sturns) was _____ American. (172)

4.81. In using the Internet to communicate with voters, the benefit of low _____ must be weighed against important problems. (176)

4.82. Financial contributions received by state officeholders must be disclosed to the Texas _____ Commission. (179)

4.83. Texas is only one of six states with no _____ on political campaign contributions (except for some judicial races). (180)

4.84. One result of public funding of elections would be to put challengers on a more equal financial footing with _____. (180)

F. Completion Questions on Readings (with textbook page numbers)

4.85. At the Texas Republican Party's 2002 convention, critics of state chair Susan Weddington made an unsuccessful attempt to place _____ limits on her office. (186)

4.86. At the Republican Party's 2002 convention, delegates identified with the Christian Right enthusiastically endorsed a resolution calling on the GOP's state representatives to choose a new House_____ in a secret caucus. (188)

4.87. Paul Burka is of the opinion that Texas Democrats overestimated
_____ turnout for the 2002 election. (190)

4.88. In painting a dismal future for Texas Democrats, Paul Burka concludes that all
they can do is wait for Republicans to make a _____. (192)

G. Essay Questions (with textbook page numbers)

1. Describe former obstacles to voting in the Lone Star State. (136–138)

2   Explain how voting has been democratized in Texas through federal voting
rights legislation and state regulations concerning voter qualifications, voter
registration, and early voting. (138–144)

3. Write an essay entitled "Texas Primaries." In this essay, describe the scheduling, administration, and financing of the Lone Star State's system for nominating Republican and Democratic candidates. (144–147)

4. Write an essay entitled "General and Special Elections in Texas." In this essay, discuss election schedules, selection and duties of election officials, and
procedures involved in administering elections. (148–152)

5. Write an essay entitled "Political Party Structure in Texas: Temporary and
Permanent Organizations." In this essay, describe the party convention system
and explain the principal functions of precinct chairs at the lowest level and
executive committees at higher levels. (152–158)

6. Write an essay on "Political Ideology in Texas Today." (158–160)

7. Prepare an outline identifying significant events and important people in the
political history of Texas from the 1840s to the early years of the twenty-first
century. (160–166)

8. Identify Texas's two major political parties and three "third parties," and
comment on their strengths and weaknesses today. (166–170)

7. Describe the impact of Latino and African American voters on Texas politics
in recent years, and comment on the prospects for greater ethnic and racial influences on the political affairs of the state in the years ahead. (170–173)

8. Explain why Texas women have begun to play more important roles as voters
and candidates, and comment on their prospects for exercising even greater
political influence in the future. (173–174)

9. Write an essay entitled "Campaigns and the Importance of Money in Texas
Politics." In your essay, discuss problems in conducting campaigns, ideas for
campaign reform, and the issue of campaign finance. (175–180)

10. Although most Americans do not make campaign contributions (especially
children), per capita amounts provide data for interesting comparisons of the
12 states in the How Do We Compare table on page 179 of this chapter. Divide the contribution amount for each state by the state's total population as

provided in the How Do We Compare table on page 16 of Chapter 1. Then
rank the states in descending order of per capita contributions. Other interesting comparisons can be made by using data for voting-age populations, registered voters, or votes cast in statewide elections,

III. *Applying Your Knowledge*

A.   **Outside Readings and Cartoons**

1. From the endnotes for this chapter or from the updated bibliography of selected sources accessible through the Houghton Mifflin Political Science
   home page (politicalscience.college.hmco.com), choose a magazine article or
   journal article and write a summary of it.
2. From the endnotes for this chapter or from the updated bibliography of selected sources accessible through the Houghton Mifflin Political Science
   home page (politicalscience.college.hmco.com), choose a book and write a
   summary of one of its chapters.
3. Find a newspaper editorial that relates to the politics of elections and parties
   in Texas. Summarize that editorial, and explain why you agree or disagree
   with the writer's point of view.
4. Find a newspaper article concerning the politics of parties and elections in
   Texas. Summarize the article, and describe what you do like and/or do not like
   about this piece of reporting.
5. Interpret one of this chapter's cartoons (or another cartoon concerning parties
   and/or elections), and explain why you agree or disagree with the cartoonist's
   point of view.
6. Explore two or more of the web sites listed among sources for this chapter.
   Then select one site and write a brief note outlining how its information contributes to your understanding of the politics of Texas elections and parties.

B.   **Internet Research Project**

Objectives

1. To examine websites maintained by the two major political parties in Texas
   (Republican and Democrat) and one of the state's "third" parties (Libertarian).
2. To enhance student knowledge of the concept of ideology through completing
   an on-line survey.
3. To introduce students to use of multiple web sites for conducting political research.
4 To understand the term "favorites/bookmarks list."

5. To help students become more efficient in using favorites or bookmarks lists.

URLs.   http://www.texasgop.org
         http://www.txdemocrats.org
         http://www.lptexas.org
         http://www.lptx.org

Description of the Sites Internet sites are maintained by the Democratic, Republican, Libertarian, and other political parties active in Texas. These web sites serve several purposes: they supply news to party members about party affairs; they provide information about party rules, leadership, and platforms; they attempt to recruit new members; and they try to raise funds.

The Internet is a dynamic, ever-changing environment. If any of the links and instructions need to be adjusted, consult the textbook's web site for updates of this exercise (http://college.hmco.com/polisci/brown/prac_tex_pol/12e/students/index.html).

Use of Information In these exercises you will learn about three of Texas's political parties. In addition, you will complete a survey that will help enhance your knowledge about ideology.

1. Go to the website (www.texasgop.org) for the home page of the Republican Party of Texas.
    a. Click the button labeled "Leadership."
    b. Then click "Party Officers" to find that the name of the chairman of the Texas Republican party is _____.
    c. Go back to the Republican Party of Texas home page and click on "Links." Then click "County Party Web Sites." If you are a Texan, select your home county if it is listed; otherwise, select the county where your college or university is located or another county. The name of the selected county is _____ and the Democratic county chair is

        _____.

2. Go to the Texas Democratic Party's web site (www.txdemocrats.org).
    a. Click the button labeled "Party and Elected Officials." On that page, click "State Officers."
    b. The name of the chair of the Texas Democratic Party is

        _____.
    c. Click "County Chairs." As directed by Instruction 2 above, select a county and search alphabetically for that county. Who is the Republican Party chair in the county? _____

3. Go to the Libertarian Party's website (www.lptexas.org).
   a. Click the "Leadership" link. What is the name of the Chair of the Texas Libertarian Party? _____
   b. Click "County Parties" and then click "List of County Chairs." Next, click on "List of All Records by County" and on "Display Selected List." Scroll down to the name of the county, if it is listed. What is the name of the county chair of the Texas Libertarian party?

      _____

4. To take a survey that should help you to understand ideology, go to www.lptx.org and scroll down to "Philosophy." Then click "World's Smallest Political Quiz." Take the quiz and click "Score It." On the results page you will find the definition of what the quiz identifies as your philosophy, along with definitions of four other philosophies. List these five philosophies and provide definitions:

   a. _____
      _____
      _____

   b. _____
      _____
      _____

   c. _____
      _____
      _____

   d. _____
      _____
      _____

   e. _____
      _____
      _____

Internet Research Tip You might want to be able to go back and examine the information on one of these web sites you visited during this exercise. If you want to be able to refer to it quickly, you can create a bookmarks or favorites list (the name will depend on your web browser). You can create lists of sites that you use frequently or want to be able to find again. Sometimes your web browser may include preset items to help promote the web browser company's products. These can be deleted. Most web experts recommend that you save URLs that interest you the first time you see them. It is often difficult to return to a site at a later date, because you may not be able to recall how you got there the first time. If you find that a web site is no longer useful or of interest to you, it can always be deleted. To reach a site that has been added to your bookmarks or favorites list, all you have to do is click on the site on your list and you will be connected.

Answers

True-False: Text	Multiple-Choice: Text	Multiple-Choice: Readings
4.1. T	4.31. a	4.61. d
4.2. T	4.32. d	4.62. b
4.3. F	4.33. b	4.63. c
4.4. F	4.34. d	4.64. c
4.5. T	4.35. a	
4.6. F	4.36. a	Completion: Text
4.7. F	4.37. d	
4.8. T	4.38. a	4.65. white
4.9. T	4.39. d	4.66. registration
4.10. F	4.40. c	4.67. turnout
4.11. T	4.41. b	4.68. Early
4.12. T	4.42. b	4.69. convention
4.13. F	4.43. a	4.70. March
4.14. T	4.44. c	4.71. touchscreen
4.15. T	4.45. d	4.72. commissioners
4.16. T	4.46. b	4.73. booth
4.17. T	4.47. d	4.74. temporary
4.18. T	4.48. a	4.75. permanent
4.19. F	4.49. a	4.76. government
4.20. F	4.50. c	4.77. dog
4.21. F	4.51. b	4.78. Reform
4.22. T	4.52. d	4.79. Crystal
4.23. T	4.53. c	4.80. African
4.24. F	4.54. a	4.81. cost
4.25. T	4.55. b	4.82. Ethics
4.26. F	4.56. a	4.83. limits
	4.57. a	4.84. incumbents
ʾe-False: Readings	4.58 c	
	4.59. b	Completion: Readings
T	4.60. b	
		4.85. term
		4.86. speaker
		4.87. Hispanic
		4.88. mistake

CHAPTER FIVE

The Politics of Interest Groups

A. Performance Objectives

After studying and reviewing the text and readings in this chapter, you will be able to:

1. Define the term *interest group* and distinguish between an interest group and a political party.
2. Explain why interest groups have grown in number and importance in Texas.
3. Summarize significant details concerning the organizational patterns, membership, and leadership in interest groups.
4. Classify interest groups and give examples of each classification.
5. Identify power groups and explain their influence on Texas politics.
6. Identify activities and techniques used by lobbyists to influence policymakers.
7. Discuss the regulation of interest groups in Texas politics.
8. Identify factors that affect interest group power and influence in Texas politics.

B. Overview of the Text (pp. 194-216)

Through group action, efforts are made to influence government officials who make and implement public policy. As a rule, political action by a group is more effective than that of an individual.

Interest Groups in the Political Process (pp. 194-196). Interest groups, as well as political parties, seek to influence the selection of government officials and the decisions that they make. Sometimes called *pressure groups*, interest groups are organized to make public officials take policy actions preferred by interest-group members. The Independent Colleges and Universities of Texas (ICUT), for example, pressures the Texas Legislature against reduction of funding for Tuition Equalization Grants that benefit students in private institutions of higher education.

Political parties focus on gaining control of government in order to achieve party goals. In contrast, interest groups seek to influence the policy decisions of whomever is elected to public office. Interest groups provide representation for economic and social elements that are not represented directly in government. Such organizations can provide functional representation that supplements the geographic representation provided by elected officials.

The ability of interest groups to wield influence is enhanced by decentralized structures of government in a federal system that features national, state, and local levels. Also of importance is the fact that governing power is divided among legislative, executive, and judicial branches. In addition, decentralized political parties, wherein cohesion often is lacking, enhance the strength of interest groups.

Organization of Interest Groups (pp. 196-198). In Texas, as elsewhere in the United States, interest groups exhibit a wide variety of organizational patterns. Some are highly centralized but others are decentralized. Prosperous, well-educated people tend to be more active in interest groups than persons with less wealth and education. As a rule, the larger a group's membership, the greater the probability that group policy will be made by a few leaders. These leaders are likely to be people who make large financial contributions, can spend time on organizational work, and have desired personality traits.

Classification of Interest Groups (pp. 198-205). There are different types of interest groups: economic (business organizations, labor unions), professional (dentists, lawyers), racial and ethnic (African Americans and Latinos), women's, public interest (consumer, environmental, civil rights), public officer and employee (city attorneys, workers in the state bureaucracy), and religious (church denominations and other faith-based organizations).

Political power of interest groups varies greatly, but Texas legislators have identified the following as being among the most powerful: trade associations of oil and gas, insurance, and chemical companies; professional associations of physicians, lawyers, and teachers; labor unions; and organizations representing realtors, truckers, brewers, automobile dealers, and bankers.

Interest-Group Activities (pp. 205-206). In Texas political life, interest groups engage in various activities, some of which overlap those of political parties. They are involved in recruiting candidates for public office, defining conflict and shaping consensus on issues, and providing outlets for citizens who desire to influence the policymaking process.

Techniques of Interest Groups (pp. 206-212). Much of any interest group's political work is done by lobbyists. Some lobbyists are former legislators or have held other public offices. A lobbyist's objective is to persuade policymakers to act as an interest group wants. When approaching a policymaker, a lobbyist identifies the group he or she represents, defines the interest, makes clear what action is desired and why, answers questions, and provides information needed for making a decision. Additional lobbying practices include providing entertainment and other personal favors, as well as persuading a decision maker that the group's goals have broad-based public support.

In addition to lobbying, techniques employed for exercising group power include electioneering, campaign financing, and even bribery and other illegal practices. Electioneering efforts involve publicizing the political records of incumbent candidates, providing candidates with group membership information and mailing lists, and encouraging voter turnout to support a group's preferred candidates. Political action committees (PACs) have come to play a very important role in raising and contributing campaign money that helps favored candidates win nominations and elections. Bribery is the crudest interest-group technique, and it is prohibited by law.

Regulation of Interest Group Politics (pp. 213-214). Established in 1991, the Texas Ethics Commission registers lobbyists and enforces state laws regulating lobbyists' activities and requiring periodic financial reports. Nevertheless, the relationship between campaign contributions by interest groups and policy decisions by elected officials persists.

Interest-Group Power and Public Policy (p. 215). In analyzing group influence, many scholars have explained that it is determined by size of membership, degree of membership unity, amount of financial resources, and quality of leadership. Others emphasize that group influence tends to vary inversely with the strength of a state's political parties. Research indicates that strong parties are found in densely populated, highly industrialized states with high levels of per capita wealth and formal education. Some scholars have noted that interest-group effectiveness is related to harmony between group aims and community beliefs, representation of groups within the structure of government, and the power of government officials.

Although Texas is wealthy, heavily urbanized, and highly industrialized, its one-party tradition and its weak, uncoordinated governmental institutions have encouraged interest-group influence. Furthermore, Texas interest groups have identified with important elements of the state's culture: free enterprise and self-reliance. Consequently, some Texans are more likely to trust lobbyists than to trust government officials. One must not assume, however, that all decisions of Texas's public officials are dictated by interest groups.

Pinpointing Political Power (pp. 215-216). Determining which interest groups, political leaders, or individuals have the most power is difficult. Likewise, magnitudes of political influence vary, depending on the issue involved. Experience indicates, however, that unorganized citizens are ill prepared to oppose organized interest groups.

Looking Ahead (p. 216). Interest groups influence policy decisions at all levels of government, within the three departments (legislative, executive, and judicial), and among members of the state's bureaucracy.

C.   Key Terms and Concepts (with textbook page numbers)

interest group (194)
NAACP v. *Alabama* (195)
right of association (195)
decentralized government (196)
organizational pattern (197)
group leadership (198)
economic interest group (199)
business organization (199)
labor organization (199)
professional group (201)
public officer and employee group (202)
social interest group (202)

racial and ethnic groups (202)
women's organization (203)
religious-based group (203)
public interest group (203)
power group (204)
interest group technique (206)
lobbying (207)
electioneering (209)
political action committee (PAC) (210)
Texas Ethics Commission (213)
political influence of interest groups (215)

D.   Overview of the Readings (pp. 219-228)

5.1. "PGA Village" by Diane M. Duesterhoeft (pp. 219-223)

On 9 March 2001, Governor Perry signed S.B. 1629 authorizing Cibolo Canyon Conservation and Improvement District No. 1. This district covered nearly 2,900 acres of land belonging to the Lumbermen's Investment Corporation (LIC).

Though the land is located outside the city limits of San Antonio, S.B. 1629 specified that a city ordinance approving a development project would be required. Such an ordinance was passed and a contract was negotiated with the Professional Golfers Association of America (PGA) for building a 500-bed resort hotel, two golf courses, and 100,000 square feet of commercial office space, along with 4,000 homes, apartments, and condos. Opponents insisted the project would endanger San Antonio's water supply, destroy wildlife habitat, encroach on an area sacred to Native Americans, and amount to a tax giveaway. After grassroots organizations mounted a petition drive for the purpose of forcing the city council to repeal the ordinance, PGA America announced its withdrawal from the deal. The ordinance was repealed, but the special taxing district was replaced with a nonannexation agreement between LIC and the city of San Antonio.

Although COPS and Metro Alliance pressured LIC into accepting a living wage requirement, other groups continued to oppose PGA Village and demanded that San Antonio's voters should have an opportunity to vote on it. At the time this article was written, the outcome was still in doubt because PGA America was undecided about its participation. Nevertheless, this affair does illustrate how grassroots organizations can have an impact on public policy.

5.2. "Political Watchdogs on Patrol" by Jay Root (pp. 223-225)

Late in 2002, Texas Republicans and business lobbyists are characterizing watchdog and consumer advocate groups as tools of the Democrats, used to thwart the GOP legislative agenda. Although leaders of these groups say they may have more in common with the Democratic Party, they note that there were significant policy disagreements when Democrats controlled state government. Further, they point out that on some issues they have received GOP support. Thus, leaders of watchdog and consumer advocate groups discount their critics' accusations of political favoritism.

5.3. "Taking Part in the Texas Municipal League's Lobbying Efforts: A Dozen Golden Rules for Grass Roots Involvement" (pp. 225-228)

Lobbying the Texas Legislature is an important function of the Texas Municipal League (TML), but staff personnel cannot do it alone. This article offers twelve "rules" of lobbying that municipal officials should follow when they supplement TML's efforts to influence legislators: (1) stay well informed, (2) put someone in charge, (3) get personally acquainted, (4) know your legislator's staff, (5) respond to the League's requests for assistance, (6) be able to act quickly, (7) express yourself, (8) write letters carefully and thoughtfully, (9) keep the League staff informed, (10) recognize their problems, (11) say thanks, and (12) do Unto Others...

II. *Testing Your Knowledge*

A. True-False Questions on Text Material (with textbook page numbers)

_____ 5.1. As a general rule, groups are more successful in achieving political goals than are individuals acting alone. (194)

_____ 5.2. Dispersal of power within branches or departments of government enhances an interest group's chances of success in influencing policymakers. (196)

_____ 5.3.   Texas voters consistently vote in accordance with their commitment to
ideological beliefs. (196)

_____ 5.4.   In Texas and other parts of the United States, a janitor is just as likely
as a lawyer or other professional person to be a member of an interest
group. (197)

_____ 5.5.   People who make the largest financial contributions to an interest
group's organization tend to have the greatest influence over its decisions. (197-198)

_____ 5.6.   Although it is a highly industrialized state, Texas has a relatively small
number of labor union members. (200)

_____ 5.7.   The NAACP is an effective social interest group. (202)

_____ 5.8.   Issues with which the Christian Coalition is actively involved include
prayer in public schools, abortion, and homosexuality. (203)

_____ 5.9.   Common Cause is an example of a religious-based interest group.
(204)

_____ 5.10. When an interest group serves as an outlet for discussion of questions
of public interest, it is helping to develop conflict or consensus. (205)

_____ 5.11. It is not unusual for lobbyists to provide free liquor, wine, or beer to
public officials. (209)

_____ 5.12. Interest groups place issue advertisements on TV broadcasts in order
to influence public opinion. (209)

_____ 5.13. Political action committees (PACs) may raise funds but are prohibited
by Texas law from contributing any money to candidates for public office. (210)

_____ 5.14. The Texas Ethics Commission enforces legal standards for lobbyists
and public officials. (213)

_____ 5.15. Unity among members of an interest group tends to increase the
group's political influence. (215)

B.   True-False Questions on Readings (with textbook page numbers)

_____ 5.16. The PGA Village project was launched because there are no golf
courses within an hour's drive of San Antonio. (219)

_____ 5.17. The Edwards Aquifer Recharge Zone (ERZ) is the sole source of
drinking water for most of San Antonio. (220)

_____ 5.18. Texans for Public Justice tracks the influence of corporate money in
politics. (224)

_____ 5.19. Consumers Union, the publisher of *Consumer Reports,* gets the bulk of its operating revenue from big-business interest groups. (225)

_____ 5.20. According to the Texas Municipal League (TML), a mayor is the only city official who should be involved in legislative communications. (225)

_____ 5.21. The Texas Municipal League suggests that a letter written to a legislator should explain a city's stance on as many pending bills as possible in order to maximize its impact. (227)

C. Multiple-Choice Questions on Text Material (with textbook page numbers)

_____ 5.22. An interest group is sometimes called a (194)

     a. government group.
     b. constitutional group.
     c. pressure group.
     d. judicial group.

_____ 5.23. The principal objective of interest groups is to (195)

     a. influence government officials, regardless of their party affiliation, in making and implementing policies.
     b. nominate interest-group members for public office.
     c. elect interest-group members to public office.
     d. recruit interest-group leaders to fill party offices.

_____ 5.24. Interest groups provide a system of (195)

     a. geographic representation.
     b. territorial representation.
     c. functional representation.
     d. symbolic representation.

_____ 5.25. The development of interest groups was greatly facilitated by the U.S. Supreme Court's decision in *NAACP* v. *Alabama* that recognized the right of association as part of the right of freedom of (195)

     a. religion.
     b. press.
     c. assembly.
     d. speech.

_____ 5.26. A decentralized party system tends to (196)

    a. discourage the formation of interest groups.
    b. magnify opportunities for effective action by interest groups.
    c. mobilize citizens against interest groups.
    d. maximize conflict among rival interest groups.

_____ 5.27. Among centralized interest-group organizations operating in Texas, one finds (197)

    a. the Libertarian Party.
    b. the Texas Association of Businesses and Chambers of Commerce.
    c. labor unions affiliated with the AFL-CIO.
    d. the National Rifle Association.

_____ 5.28. The Texas Association of Engineering Geologists is (201)

    a. a professional group.
    b. an organized labor group.
    c. an ethnic group.
    d. an economic group.

_____ 5.29. The Christian Coalition of Texas primarily engages in political action in support of (203)

    a. the Democratic Party.
    b. the Republican Party.
    c. the Libertarian Party.
    d. the Green Party.

_____ 5.30. The Texas Faith Network was formed to combat the activities of the (203)

    a. Communist Party.
    b. Roman Catholic Church.
    c. Baptist General Convention of Texas.
    d. Christian Coalition.

_____ 5.31. An interest group that focuses on issues involving environmental, consumer, political participation, or civil rights affairs is most likely to be classified as a(n) (203-204)

    a. business group.
    b. professional group.
    c. public-interest group.
    d. economic-interest group.

_____ 5.32. According to Texas legislators, the most influential interest groups operating in the Lone Star State include (204)

    a. public interest groups.
    b. ethnic interest groups.
    c. business-oriented trade associations.
    d. associations of university professors.

_____ 5.33. The Texas Medical Association is a an interest group with (205)

    a. half a million members.
    b. a poor record for passing its agenda items.
    c. an unskilled lobbying team.
    d. a well-organized grassroots network.

_____ 5.34. The first task of the lobbyist is to (207)

    a. bribe selected government officials.
    b. mobilize voters.
    c. influence public opinion.
    d. gain access to legislators and other government decision-makers.

_____ 5.35. Among the main techniques of lobbyists is (207)

    a. personal communication.
    b. bribery.
    c. blackmail.
    d. computer fraud.

_____ 5.36. A professional lobbyist representing an interest group will rely heavily on a grassroots network that can be employed to impress legislators with (207)

    a. the image of broad public support for the group's goals.
    b. the danger of personal harm if the group's will is thwarted.
    c. the opportunity for personal enrichment if the group's demands are granted.
    d. their own weakness and incompetence.

_____ 5.37. Texas statutes prohibit financial contributions by corporations and labor unions to (210)

    a. law schools.
    b. political science research institutes at state universities.
    c. candidates for public office.
    d. nonpolitical public service organizations.

_____ 5.38. PACs raise funds and distribute campaign contributions to candidates who (210)

    a. are prohibited by law from using personal funds to cover campaign expenses.

    b. are sympathetic to a PAC's cause.

    c. are most deserving because of a record of public service.

    d. do not receive financial support from a political party.

_____ 5.39. The Sharpstown Bank scandal in the 1970s involved (212)

    a. Governor Dolph Briscoe.

    b. Lieutenant Governor Bill Hobby.

    c. House Speaker Gus Mutscher.

    d. House Speaker Bill Clayton.

_____ 5.40. Ethics legislation enacted by the 72nd Texas Legislature in 1991 (213)

    a. bans all lobbying activities.

    b. places an annual cap on lobbyist-provided food and drinks for legislators.

    c. allows one lobbyist-paid vacation trip per legislator per year.

    d. limits honoraria paid to legislators to $1,000 per speech.

_____ 5.41. The Texas Ethics Commission's web site lists the names of lobbyists and (213)

    a. members of their staff.

    b. their spouses.

    c. their clients.

    d. their bankers.

_____ 5.42. Generally, states that are urbanized and industrialized have (215)

    a. strong interest groups and weak political parties.

    b. strong political parties and relatively weak interest groups.

    c. strong political parties and strong interest groups.

    d. weak interest groups and weak political parties.

_____ 5.43. Texas is best characterized as a state with (215)

    a. strong interest groups and weak political parties.

    b. strong political parties and weak interest groups.

    c. strong political parties and strong interest groups.

    d. weak interest groups and weak political parties.

_____ 5.44. The authors of *Practicing Texas Politics* suggest that the strength of interest groups in Texas is, in part, a result of (215)

    a. the influence of ethnic minorities.
    b. a predisposition of Texans to mistrust government.
    c. a strong socialist influence.
    d. a pronounced lack of self-reliance among Texans.

_____ 5.45. When dealing with public issues, organized interest groups often put the unorganized Texas citizenry (216)

    a. at a great disadvantage.
    b. on an equal footing.
    c. on a slightly unequal footing.
    d. at a modest disadvantage.

D. Multiple-Choice Questions on Readings (with textbook page numbers)

_____ 5.46. At the heart of the controversy concerning PGA Village is the concern of many San Antonio residents for the city's (219-220)

    a. water supply.
    b. ozone levels.
    c. traffic congestion.
    d. crime rate.

_____ 5.47. In an effort to kill the PGA Village project, opponents launched (221-222)

    a. a campaign of terrorism against members of San Antonio's city council.
    b. a petition drive.
    c. a third-party movement.
    d. a rival project to build municipal golf courses.

_____ 5.48. Texas Republicans accuse critics representing consumer groups as being fronts for personal-injury trial lawyers and (224)

    a. Communists.
    b. Libertarians.
    c. Greens.
    d. Democrats.

_____ 5.49. Texans for Public Justice receives most of its funding from (225)

    a. foundations.

    b. the Democratic Party.

    c. the National Rifle Association.

    d. the Republican Party.

_____ 5.50. According to the Texas Municipal League, persons wishing to influence a legislator should also get to know (226)

    a. the legislator's spouse.

    b. as many lobbyists as possible.

    c. members of the legislator's staff.

    d. House and Senate doorkeepers.

_____ 5.51. According to the Texas Municipal League, the best place to express disagreement with a legislator is in (228)

    a. a private conference.

    b. a public forum.

    c. a newspaper ad.

    d. a mass demonstration by employees or interest group members.

E.   Completion Questions on Text Material (with textbook page numbers)

5.52. Interest groups try to build _____ with other groups whose interests are identical or closely related on one or more issues. (195)

5.53. An interest-group organization is almost invariably composed of an active minority and a _____ majority. (197)

5.54. LULAC is one of the groups representing _____ in Texas. (202)

5.55. The League of Women Voters is an example of a _____ organization that promotes greater political participation and public understanding of governmental issues. (203)

5.56. Cecile Richards played a leading role in organizing the Texas Freedom Network to oppose the _____ Coalition. (203)

5.57. Texans for Public Justice is an example of a _____ interest group. (204)

5.58. Interest groups that have been politically influential over a long period of time are often referred to as "_____ players." (204)

5.59. The city in which Texas's powerful interest groups are likely to have their headquarters is _____. (204)

5.60   Among all states in the United States, Texas ranks second to
_____ in the number of registered lobby groups. (207)

5.61.   Pressure on legislators and other decision makers from a grassroots network of
organization members and sympathizers is a technique often referred to as
_____ lobbying. (209)

5.62.   Former legislators and other government officials who leave government service
and immediately begin lobbying are referred to as "revolving-_____"
lobbyists. (214)

5.63.   As a result of unsuccessful efforts to reform campaign financing in the Lone Star
State, columnist Mollie Ivins has stated, "Texas is the _____ Frontier
of campaign financing." (214)

F.   Completion Questions on Readings (with textbook page numbers)

5.64.   The San Antonio controversy over PGA Village began on 9 March 2001, when a
_____ was filed in the Texas Senate. (219)

5.65.   American Indians at the San Antonio Colonial Missions opposed any development
in the area near Cibolo Creek because it had always been deemed
_____. (220)

5.66.   Reggie James, head of a local branch of the Consumers Union, stated that it
doesn't matter whether Democrats or Republicans control the Texas Legislature,
because "_____ has always dominated everything." (224)

5.67.   Common Cause director Suzie Woodford notes that her organization's motto is
"No permanent friends, no permanent _____." (225)

5.68.   Although a telephone call or letter can be productive for influencing a legislator,
the Texas Municipal League suggests that personal _____
contact is the most effective approach. (227)

5.69.   The Texas Municipal League recommends that legislators should be
_____ regularly and publicly for their work, support, and votes.
(228).

G.   Essay Questions (with textbook page numbers)

1.   Write an essay on the following topic: "The Importance of Interest Groups in
State Government." Explain why interest groups have been created, identify
differences from and similarities to political parties, and discuss reasons why
interest groups have proliferated in Texas. (194-196)

2. Write an essay on "Organization of Interest Groups" in which you describe organizational patterns, membership characteristics, and leadership (196-198)
3. Name two Texas organizations within each of the following categories: labor unions, trade associations, professional groups, and public interest groups. Then explain why you would tend to support or oppose the activities of these organizations. (199-204)
4. Describe the lobbying activities of interest groups along with two other interest-group techniques. Comment on positive and/or negative aspects of these activities, and speculate on your own possibilities for interest-group participation in the years ahead. (206-212)
5. Write an essay on Regulation of Interest Groups in Texas." In your essay, explain why you think there is too much regulation or insufficient regulation. (213-214)
6. Write an essay entitled "Interest-Group Power in Texas." In your essay, explain why interest groups are powerful in Texas; and speculate on the future of interest groups in the Lone Star State. Indicate why you believe that some will grow stronger, others will become weaker, and some will retain their current status. (215-216)
7. Using data in the How Do We Compare box on at the bottom of page 211, rank the 8 states in descending order according to percentage of PAC contributions given to Democrats in the 2002 congressional election. Then note the geographic region for each state: Southwest: Oklahoma, Texas, and New Mexico; South: Arkansas, Florida, and Louisiana; Northeast: New York; and Pacific Coast, California. What regional differences and similarities do you observe?

III. *Applying Your Knowledge*

A.   Outside Readings and Cartoons

1. From the endnotes for this chapter or from the updated bibliography of selected sources accessible through the Houghton Mifflin Political Science home page (politicalscience.college.hmco.com), choose a magazine article or a journal article and write a summary of it.
2. From the endnotes for this chapter or from the updated bibliography of selected sources accessible through the Houghton Mifflin Political Science home page (politicalscience.college.hmco.com), choose a book and write a summary of one of its chapters.
3. In a Texas newspaper, find an editorial that relates to the politics of interest groups in Texas. Summarize that editorial, and explain why you agree or disagree with the writer's point of view.

4. Find a newspaper article concerning interest-group politics. Summarize the article, and describe what you do and/or do not like about this piece of reporting.

5. Interpret one of this chapter's cartoons (or another cartoon related to interest groups), and explain why you agree or disagree with the cartoonist's point of view.

6. Explore two or more of the web sites listed among sources for this chapter. Then select one site and write a brief note outlining how its information contributes to your understanding of the politics of interest groups in Texas.

B.   Internet Research Project

Objectives

1. To explain the functions of the Texas Ethics Commission.
2. To enhance student understanding of the number of lobbyists and special interests in the state.
3. To develop an understanding of the domain name system (DNS).

URL. http://www.ethics.state.tx.us

Description of the Site. The Texas Ethics Commission maintains this web site. Created in 1991 by the 72nd Legislature, the commission has several responsibilities. Among its duties are assuring accurate and timely filings of personal financial statements by elected and appointed officials and certain agency administrators, supervising the conduct of elected and appointed officials and all state employees to insure that they are in compliance with state ethics laws, overseeing filings and expenditures of political action committees, and monitoring political contributions, expenditures, and political advertising.

In 2000, the Ethics Commission became responsible for monitoring and enforcing electronic filing of campaign expenditures and contributor lists for all statewide candidates and officeholders, as well as state legislators and members of the State Board of Education. Additionally, this appointed commission regulates lobbyist registration and activities.

Individuals who directly contact a legislator or bureaucrat to influence a decision about legislation, rule making, or related activities are lobbyists. Most of these individuals must register with the Ethics Commission. Registration laws are complex. They are found in Chapter 305 of the *Texas Government Code,* which is available on this site. Additionally, individuals with questions about how ethics laws and regulations should be interpreted can ask the commission for an opinion or interpretation. These opinions may be accessed at this site.

Under a legislative mandate, Ethics Commission staff members have developed a database of information filed with the agency which is available on the commission's web site. Information is categorized in several ways. There are al-phabetized lists of (1) all registered lobbyists and their clients and (2) all clients and their lobbyists. There is also a list of all lobbyists sorted by subject matter. In addi-tion, information about political action committees and political campaign contribu-tions and expenditures is available.

The internet is a dynamic, ever-changing environment. If any of the links and instructions need to be adjusted please consult the textbook web site for updates of this exercise (http://college.hmco.com/polisci/brown/prac_tex_pol/12e/students/index.html).

Use of Information. Lobbyists in the state of Texas represent many interests that range from local governments to abortion rights activists to businesses. Some lob-byists represent more than one group. Many companies and interest groups employ more than one lobbyist.

1. Go to the Ethics Commission's home page. In the section labeled "Disclosure Filing" click on "Filer Lists." Then click on "Lobby Lists" to access the index for the different databases for lobbyists.

2. Locate the most current section labeled "List of Registered Lobbyists with Clients, sorted by Clients." Click on Part III (M-S). Clients can be (a) compa-nies, (b)individuals, or (c) interest groups such as those listed in *Practicing Texas Politics,* p. 200 (Table 5.1), p. 201 (Table 5.2), and p. 204 (Table 5.3).

    a. Locate one company; list its name and the number of lobbyists represent-ing it.

    _____

    b. Locate one individual; list that individual's name and the number of lob-byists representing him or her.

    _____

    c. Locate one interest group; list that interest group's name and the number of lobbyists representing it.

    _____

3. Identify one lobbyist, by name, representing each of the clients listed above.

    a. _____

    b. _____

    c. _____

4. Return to the page labeled "List of Registered Lobbyists" and check the "List of Registered Lobbyists (without client information," which is sorted by lobbyists. The list is alphabetized by the lobbyists' last names. Go to the correct part for each lobbyist you have listed in #3. Determine how many other clients each of the lobbyists has.

a. _____

b. _____

c. _____

Internet Research Tip. You may have noticed that the URL for the Texas Ethics Commission ends with **state.tx.us**. This part of the commission's URL is the result of the domain name system (DNS). The DNS is a way of organizing servers on the Internet by the purposes of their organizations or their geographical location. It is a translation of the Internet Protocol (IP) address, or series of numbers, assigned to each computer (or host) on the Internet. Domain names translate the numbers into more easily remembered words and numbers.

The URL for all Texas state governmental units and agencies ends with **state.tx.us**. This designation is a geographical domain which shows that the governmental unit is in the United States. Community colleges in the state also use a geographical domain that includes **cc.tx.us** in their URLs. However, senior colleges and universities throughout the United States generally end their URLs with **.edu**. This designation is called an organizational domain. Both the geographical and organizational domains are top-level domains (TLDs). All URLs that end with the top-level domain of **.edu** are educational institutions. Other top-level organizational domains include **.org** (nonprofit organizations), **.net** (network organizations that serve as hosts for individual users), **.com** (for-profit entities), **.int** (international organizations), **.gov** (federal governmental entities), and **.mil** (military). These top-level organizational domains are consistent for individuals and organizations within the United States. Foreign servers use different TLDs.

Answers

True-False: Text

5.1.	T
5.2.	T
5.3.	F
5.4.	F
5.5.	T
5.6.	T
5.7.	T
5.8.	T
5.9.	F
5.10.	T
5.11.	T
5.12.	T
5.13.	F
5.14.	T
5.15.	T

True-False: Readings

5.16.	F
5.17.	T
5.18.	T
5.19.	F
5.20.	F
5.21.	F

Multiple-Choice: Text

5.22.	c
5.23.	a
5.24.	c
5.25.	c
5.26.	b
5.27.	d
5.28.	a
5.29.	b
5.30.	d
5.31.	c
5.32.	c
5.33.	d
5.34.	d
5.35.	a
5.36.	a
5.37.	c
5.38.	b
5.39.	c
5.40.	b
5.41.	c
5.42.	b
5.43.	a
5.44.	b
5.45.	a

Multiple-Choice: Readings

5.46.	a
5.47.	b
5.48.	d
5.49.	a
5.50.	c
5.51.	a

Completion: Text

5.52.	coalitions
5.53.	passive
5.54.	Latinos
5.55.	nonpartisan
5.56.	Christian
5.57.	public
5.58.	repeat
5.59.	Austin
5.60.	California
5.61.	grassroots
5.62.	door
5.63.	Wild

Completion: Readings

5.64.	bill
5.65.	sacred
5.66.	business
5.67.	enemies
5.68.	face-to-face
5.69.	thanked

CHAPTER SIX

The Legislature

I. *Preparing to Study*

A. Performance Objectives

After studying and reviewing the text and readings in this chapter, you will be able to:

1. Outline the constitutional qualifications for members of the Texas House of Representatives and Senate.
2. Outline the bases of representation for the Texas House and Senate, and describe the process of redistricting.
3. Discuss all aspects of compensation for members of the Texas Legislature, including pay, per diem allowance, contingency expense allowances, and retirement pensions.
4. Profile the House and Senate memberships, including race and gender, political party affiliation, age, occupation, education, religious affiliation, and legislative experience.
5. List different types of resolutions and bills; indicate the majorities required for adopting or passing each type; and explain the purpose of each type.
6. Identify and describe the powers of the House and Senate that only relate indirectly to the lawmaking function.
7. Describe the functions and powers of the presiding officers of the House and the Senate.
8. Describe the House and Senate committee systems.
9. Identify important House and Senate caucuses, and give reasons for the existence of these caucuses.
10. Outline the steps whereby a bill becomes a law.
11. Identify various influences on the legislative process, and explain the importance of each in the making of public policy.
12. Speculate on prospects for meaningful reform of the Texas Legislature in the near future.

B.   **Overview of the Text** (pp. 230-276)

Members of the Texas Legislature are popularly elected. The laws that they enact affect the life, liberty, and property of every Texan.

A Preliminary View (pp. 230-231). The legislative process involves heated political conflict, frustrating delays, and many compromises.

Legislative Framework (pp. 231-240). Texas has a bicameral legislature. The Senate has 31 senators, who are elected for terms of four years; the House has 150 representatives, who are elected for terms of two years. Regular sessions, lasting not more than 140 days, begin in January of odd-numbered years. The governor calls special sessions, limited to not more than 30 days.

After every federal census taken at the beginning of each decade, the legislature is supposed to redistrict itself during the regular session of the following year. If the legislature fails to carry out this districting task, the five-member Legislative Redistricting Board must do the work. Regardless of which body does the redistricting, one or more political parties or interest groups are certain to challenge every districting plan in state and/or federal courts.

Compensation (pp. 240-242). Legislators receive an annual salary of $7,200. A per diem allowance is set by the Texas Ethics Commission. Travel and contingency expenses (such as staff salaries, postage, and office operating costs) are authorized by each chamber. The minimum retirement age is 50 for legislators who have served for 12 or more years.

Membership (pp. 243-249). U.S. citizenship, status as a qualified voter, and residence in the district for at least one year before election are constitutional requirements for all legislators. A representative must be at least 21 years of age and a senator at least 26. The minimum state-residency requirements are two years for representatives and five years for senators.

Although the numbers of Republicans, women, Latinos, and African Americans in the legislature significantly increased between 1971 and 2003, most legislators are Anglo males. Both senators and representatives are usually native Texans who have attended at least one college or university. About a third of all Texas legislators are practicing lawyers. Roman Catholic legislators constitute the most numerous religious group. Usually, the turnover rate has been between 10 and 20 percent in recent years.

Powers and Immunities (pp. 250-253). Legislative powers include authority to adopt simple resolutions involving the affairs of a single chamber and joint resolutions that require approval by both houses. Concurrent resolutions and bills must pass the House and Senate before being sent to the governor, who may sign a measure, allow it to become law without signing, or veto it. Other important powers, some of which relate only indirectly to lawmaking, include the power to propose amendments to the Texas Constitution, to exercise control over administrative agencies through appropriations and requests for reports from agency heads, to investigate any governmental matter, and to remove high-ranking executive and judicial officials. Removal power is exercised through adopting an impeachment resolution by a simple majority vote of the House and obtaining a conviction by a two-thirds majority vote of the Senate. The Texas Constitution grants legislators immunity from slander suits for statements made in the course of any legislative proceeding. During a legislative session, a legislator may not be arrested unless charged with "treason, felony, or breach of peace."

Presiding Officers (pp. 253-257). The president of the Senate is the lieutenant governor, who is popularly elected. Lieutenant Governor Rick Perry became governor after Governor George W. Bush was elected U.S. President in 2000. Subsequently, Bill Ratliff was elected by Senate members to serve as acting lieutenant governor until January 2003. Ratliff was replaced by David Dewhurst, who had been elected by Texas voters in November 2002.

State representatives elect a speaker, who serves as presiding officer of the House. Democrat Gib Lewis held that office for five terms (1983–1993); Democrat Pete Laney was elected for his first term as speaker in 1993 and served until 2003. He was replaced by Republican Tom Craddick after the GOP obtained a House majority in the November 2002 election.

Committee System (pp. 257-259). The speaker of the House and the president of the Senate name committee chairs in their respective chambers. Both presiding officers designate committee members, but the speaker's appointment power is restricted by a limited seniority system.

Legislative Caucus System (pp. 259-261). Caucuses of like-minded legislators have had a limited impact on the legislature. Democratic and Republican caucuses exist in both the House and the Senate. The Texas Conservative Coalition was organized in 1985; the liberal Legislative Study Group was organized in 1993; and racial/ethnic caucuses have been formed by both African Americans and Mexican Americans.

Procedure (pp. 262-270). The procedure through which a bill becomes a law involves introduction and first reading, assignment to a standing committee by the presiding officer, committee consideration and report, floor debate, a first vote on the second reading, and a second vote on the third reading. These actions must be taken by both houses. In the event of disagreement over an amendment added in the second house, a bill may be sent to a conference committee composed of five representatives and five senators. If the conference committee's report is accepted by both the House and Senate, the measure goes to the governor, who can sign it, allow it to become law without signature, or kill it with a veto.

Influences within the Legislative Environment (pp. 270-275). Legislators usually do not press for passage of a bill if the governor has indicated that it will be vetoed. Any legislator may request an opinion on the constitutionality of a bill from the attorney general of Texas. Most bills are affected by the influence of one or more lobbyists representing special interest groups. Although the lobby is an informal, extraconstitutional institution, lobbyists are so powerful that collectively they are called the "Third House." Registration and reporting regulations have been imposed for identifying lobbyists and publicizing certain information about the amounts of money spent for lobbying.

When the legislature is in session, the House Research Organization publishes a daily report in which important bills are analyzed. This independent research body also produces special reports on important policy issues. The Senate Research Center analyzes bills and responds to senators' requests for research and information. Serving members of both chambers is the Legislative Council, which aids in the drafting of bills, provides computer services, and serves as a research and information source. The Center for Public Policy Priorities and the Texas Public Policy Foundation are independent think tanks that provide public policy research and analysis.

Progress Toward Legislative Reform (p. 275). Although some legislative reforms have been made in recent years, there is no indication that Texans are ready for fundamental changes. And as in earlier years, well-financed lobbyists remain at the center of the lawmaking process.

Looking Ahead (pp. 275-276). As a result of the 2000 elections, Republicans kept their majority in the Senate and gained control of the House. But since the GOP leadership seeks to increase the powers of the governor, one can expect that legislative influence will decrease in the years ahead. Meanwhile, constitutional change in legislative organization is not likely.

C. Key Terms and Concepts (with textbook page numbers)

unicameral (231)

bicameral (231)

regular session (234)

special session (234)

redistricting (234)

gerrymandering (235)

single-member district (236)

multimember district (236)

simple resolution (250)

concurrent resolution (250)

joint resolution (250)

bill (251)

senatorial courtesy (252)

impeachment (253)

president of the Senate (254)

speaker (255)

substantive committee (257)

procedural committee (258)

select committee (259)

standing committee (259)

special committee (259)

parliamentarian (262)

companion bill (265)

ghost voting (267)

chubbing (267)

filibustering (269)

conference committee (269)

D. Overview of the Readings (pp. 280-291)

6.1. "Legislative Redistricting and Electoral Results in the 21st Century: Texas and California" by Lyle C. Brown and Jerry Wilkins (pp. 280-284)

Legislative redistricting in Texas and California, following the 2000 census, painted two different pictures of political party interaction. In Texas, neither a House nor a Senate redistricting bill was enacted. Thus, the Legislative Redistricting Board redistricted the Lone Star State's House and Senate. Subsequently, the House redistricting plan was modified by a three-member panel of federal judges; and Republicans won healthy majorities in both chambers in the 2002 election.

In California, a confluence of interests between the Democrats and Republicans led to cooperative redistricting plans for both legislative chambers. The Golden State's legislature decided to eliminate most partisan competition, making almost all legislative districts "safe," so Democrats maintained control over both the Senate and the Assembly after the 2002 election. Thus, Texas and California provide different models of legislative redistricting and different electoral results.

6.2. "Watch Him Pull a Rabbit out of Hat" by Christy Hoppe (pp. 284-287)

Ron Wilson (D-Houston) is 26-year veteran House member. He is a champion of controversial issues as diverse as school vouchers, concealed handguns, and payment of reparations to African Americans whose ancestors were slaves. This African-American legislator has intimate knowledge of rules of procedure and a long-term agenda. Even those who disagree with him politically voice admiration for his abilities and for the legislative results that he generates.

6.3. "Foundation Erred in Invoking Names" by Laylan Copelin (pp. 287-291)

The Texas Public Policy Foundation (TPPF) was criticized because of its letter to Austin lobbyists soliciting funds for the foundation's "Legislative Policy Orientation for 2003." In the opinion of some critics, this offer of an "insider's look" at upcoming legislative initiatives implied a relationship between paying $5,000 to $100,000 to the TPPF and gaining access to top-level state Republican officials. The solicitation seemed to have the endorsement of Governor Rick Perry, Lieutenant Governor-elect David Dewhurst, and House Speaker-apparent Tom Craddick. After the letter was made public, however, these officials denied that they had approved use of their names to promote the conference. Concerning the controversial letter, TPPF's government relations director stated, "We made a mistake."

II. *Testing Your Knowledge*

A. **True-False Questions on Text Material** (with textbook page numbers)

_____ 6.1. Traditionally, the legislature has been the most heavily criticized and ridiculed branch of Texas government. (230)

_____ 6.2. A Texas state senator may be expelled by a two-thirds majority vote of the membership of the Senate. (234)

_____ 6.3. Special sessions of the Texas Legislature are called by the lieutenant governor. (234)

_____ 6.4. In *Reynolds* v. *Sims* (1964), the U.S. Supreme Court held that apportionment of both houses of a bicameral state legislature must be based on population. (235)

_____ 6.5. Members of the Texas Senate have always been elected to represent single-member districts. (236)

_____ 6.6. Compensation of state legislators is *not* mentioned in the Texas Constitution. (240)

_____ 6.7. Members of the Texas Legislature are *not* covered by a state retirement program. (242)

_____ 6.8. Compared with the number of men in the Texas Legislature, the number of women is disproportionately low. (246)

_____ 6.9. Most of Texas's African-American and Latino legislators have been Democrats. (247)

_____ 6.10. In recent years, nearly all Texas state senators and representatives have had college and university degrees. (248)

_____ 6.11. Because the Texas Constitution contains a detailed requirement for separation of church and state, religion is never a factor in formulating public policy in the legislature. (248)

_____ 6.12. A concurrent resolution adopted by the legislature and signed by the governor is employed to authorize an individual to sue the state of Texas. (250)

_____ 6.13. In Texas, impeachment and removal from state office automatically result in a five-year prison sentence. (253)

_____ 6.14. The president of the Texas Senate is elected by state senators at the beginning of each regular session. (254)

_____ 6.15. The speaker is chosen by members of the Texas House of Representatives, but lobbyists try to influence this legislative election. (255)

_____ 6.16. Neither a racial caucus nor an ethnic caucus has been formed in the Texas Legislature. (261)

_____ 6.17. The "Memorial Day Massacre" took place in May 1997, when Representative Arlene Wohlgemuth raised a point of order in the House. (262)

_____ 6.18. The caption of a bill is read aloud by the parliamentarian on the first reading of a House bill. (265)

_____ 6.19. House rules require a simple majority vote to amend a bill at the third reading. (267)

_____ 6.20. Filibustering in the Texas Senate is most successful if undertaken during the last days of a legislative session. (269)

_____ 6.21. In the Texas Legislature, a conference committee is composed of five senators and ten representatives. (269)

_____ 6.22. After the end of a legislative session, the governor of Texas has only ten days, counting Sundays, in which to veto a bill. (270)

_____ 6.23. The House Research Organization produces its *Daily Floor Report* during each legislative session. (273)

B. True-False Questions on Readings (with textbook page numbers)

_____ 6.24. In 2001, both House and Senate redistricting bills were passed by the Texas Legislature. (280)

_____ 6.25. Neither an Assembly nor a Senate redistricting bill was passed by the California Legislature in 2001. (282)

_____ 6.26. Representative Ron Wilson has passed many important bills despite his ignorance of parliamentary procedure and House rules. (286)

_____ 6.27. Representative Ron Wilson claims that his bills are designed to better the lives of his inner-city constituents. (286)

_____ 6.28. The Texas Public Policy Foundation was criticized for seeking a legislative appropriation to fund its "Legislative Policy Orientation for 2003." (288-289)

_____ 6.29. The government relations director for the Texas Public Policy Foundation refused to admit that TPPF had made a mistake when it mailed to lobbyists a solicitation letter that appeared to have the endorsement of high-ranking state officials. (289)

C. Multiple-Choice Questions on Text Material (with textbook page numbers)

_____ 6.30. Compared with the regular term of office for a Texas state senator, the term of a state representative is (234)

   a.   half as long.
   b.   twice as long.
   c.   one-third as long.
   d.   of equal length.

_____ 6.31. A special session of the Texas Legislature may be called (234)

   a.   only in odd-numbered years.
   b.   whenever the speaker and the lieutenant governor choose to issue a call.
   c.   only in even-numbered years.
   d.   whenever the governor chooses to issue a call.

_____ 6.32. Failure of the Texas Legislature to redistrict during the first regular session following a decennial census brings into operation the (235)

   a.   Legislative Council.
   b.   House Research Organization.
   c.   Legislative Redistricting Board.
   d.   Sunset Advisory Commission.

6.33. Use of single-member districts for electing members of the Texas House of Representatives has (237)

    a. made election campaigns more expensive for House candidates.
    b. increased the probability that minority candidates will win House seats.
    c. reduced Republican representation in the House.
    d. reduced opportunities for personal contact between representatives and their constituents.

6.34. The per diem allowance for Texas legislators is set by (240)

    a. the Legislature.
    b. the governor.
    c. the Texas Ethics Commission.
    d. the comptroller of public accounts.

6.35. Each member of the Texas Legislature is provided with a contingency expense allowance that is used for items such as (243)

    a. food consumed during a legislative session.
    b. salaries for staff personnel.
    c. rent for an Austin apartment.
    d. medical and dental care.

6.36. Constitutional qualifications for Texas state senators and representatives differ with regard to (243)

    a. U.S. citizenship.
    b. age.
    c. voter qualifications.
    d. length of residence within the district to be represented.

6.37. From 1961 to 2001, Republican representation in the Texas Legislature (244)

    a. remained at roughly the same level.
    b. increased greatly.
    c. decreased greatly.
    d. decreased slightly.

_____ 6.38. Once elected to a seat in the Texas Legislature, there is a tendency for (248)

    a. representatives to seek a second term and for senators to retire after serving one term.

    b. senators and representatives to serve for roughly the same number of years.

    c. senators and representatives to serve until the age of 65.

    d. senators to remain in the Senate longer than representatives remain in the House.

_____ 6.39. Most appointments made by the governor of Texas must be approved by a vote of two-thirds of (252)

    a. senators and representatives present.

    b. senators present.

    c. representatives present.

    d. neither senators nor representatives.

_____ 6.40. Under terms of the Texas Constitution, impeachment charges against certain judicial and executive officials are brought by a simple majority vote of (253)

    a. senators and representatives sitting together in a joint session.

    b. representatives present.

    c. senators present.

    d. the Supreme Court.

_____ 6.41. The constitutional immunity guaranteed to Texas state senators and representatives extends to statements made during the course of a (253)

    a. judicial proceeding in a court of law.

    b. primary election campaign.

    c. floor debate in a legislative chamber.

    d. general election campaign.

_____ 6.42. In Texas, the lieutenant governor's most important function is to serve as the (254)

    a. secretary of the Senate.

    b. president of the Senate.

    c. president pro tempore of the Senate.

    d. permanent speaker pro tempore of the House.

_____ 6.43. First in line of succession in the event of the death of the governor of Texas is the (254)

    a. parliamentarian of the Senate.
    b. chief justice of the Supreme Court of Texas.
    c. speaker of the House of Representatives.
    d. lieutenant governor.

_____ 6.44. After serving as speaker for five terms (1983–1993), Gib Lewis became (256)

    a. a professor of political science at Texas Christian University.
    b. the U.S. consul in Manzanillo, Mexico.
    c. a lobbyist.
    d. a member of the Texas Board of Criminal Justice.

_____ 6.45. Chairs of standing committees and special committees in the Senate are (259)

    a. elected by members of their respective committees.
    b. appointed by the lieutenant governor.
    c. appointed by the president pro tempore of the Senate.
    d. appointed by the secretary of the Senate.

_____ 6.46. Any Texas House member may introduce a bill by filing copies with the (265)

    a. speaker.
    b. chair of the committee that has been given jurisdiction over the subject covered.
    c. permanent speaker pro tempore.
    d. chief clerk.

_____ 6.47. A bill that has passed on a second reading in the Texas House can have its third reading immediately if the House rules are suspended by a (267)

    a. simple majority vote.
    b. two-thirds majority vote.
    c. three-fourths majority vote.
    d. four-fifths majority vote.

_____ 6.48. After a Texas House bill is passed on the third reading in the House, a
               statement certifying passage is added by the (268)

    a. chief clerk.

    b. speaker of the House.

    c. reading clerk.

    d. speaker pro tempore.

_____ 6.49. Texas's political history reveals that significant reform and pressure
               for ethical conduct usually come only after (276)

    a. a presidential election.

    b. a gubernatorial election.

    c. a highly publicized scandal.

    d. widespread rioting by dissident citizens.

D.   Multiple-Choice Questions on Readings (with textbook page numbers)

_____ 6.50. After the 2001 regular legislative session, redistricting plans for the
               Texas House and Senate were prepared by the (281)

    a. Supreme Court of Texas.

    b. U.S. Supreme Court.

    c. House speaker and Senate president.

    d. Legislative Redistricting Board.

_____ 6.51. In 2001, California's Assembly and Senate districts were redrawn to
               (283)

    a. punish Democrats.

    b. punish Republicans.

    c. create "safe" seats for incumbents.

    d. guarantee litigation that would reach the U.S. Supreme Court.

_____ 6.52. Representative Ron Wilson wants to (286)

    a. give 16-year-olds the right to vote.

    b. lower the drinking age to 16.

    c. privatize all public schools.

    d. abolish the Texas lottery.

_____ 6.53. One of Representative Ron Wilson's goals is forcing (285)

    a. Austin to reopen its Robert Mueller Airport.

    b. Mexico to open its border to free trade.

    c. the descendents of African slaves to pay reparations to descendents of their former masters.

    d. airport security guards to use racial profiling to identify members of the Ku Klux Klan.

_____ 6.54. The founder of the Texas Public Policy Foundation is (290)

    a. Dr. James Leininger.

    b. Craig McDonald.

    c. Wendy Gramm.

    d. Michael Quinn Sullivan.

_____ 6.55. Because a majority of members of the Texas Legislature were expected to attend the Texas Public Policy Foundation's "Legislative Policy Orientation for 2003," it had to be open to anyone because of the state's (291)

    a. fire codes.

    b. concealed weapons law.

    c. open meetings law.

    d. right to work law.

E. Completion Questions on Text Material (with textbook page numbers)

6.56. Terms of members of the Texas House of Representatives begin in January of each _____-numbered year. (234)

6.57. Regular sessions of the Texas Legislature are limited to one every _____-numbered year. (234)

6.58. Drawing legislative district boundaries in ways that unfairly benefit a group or a political party is called _____. (235)

6.59. Rhode Island and New Hampshire are examples of states where legislators are paid salaries that are _____ than the salaries of Texas legislators. (240)

6.60. The Texas Constitution specifies that a state senator must be at least _____ years of age. (243)

6.61. The first African American elected to the Texas Senate in the twentieth century was Barbara _____. (245)

6.62. Within the metropolitan areas of Texas, Republican senators and representatives have received their strongest support from voters living in _____ areas. (247)

6.63. Ordinarily, if a Texas lawyer-legislator is retained to represent a client whose trial is set for a date during a legislative session, that legislator may obtain postponement of the trial by asking for a _____. (247)

6.64. A _____ resolution abbreviated "HR" involves action by the Texas House of Representatives only. (250)

6.65. A local bill disguised as a general bill but applying to a single unit of local government falling within a narrow range of population is called a _____ bill. (236)

6.66. To obtain information on problems requiring remedial legislation, a legislative investigating committee may _____ witnesses. (252)

6.67. As House speaker in the 73rd Legislature, Pete Laney ended the practice of bringing _____ machines into the Capitol. (256)

6.68. The ideological _____ Coalition is composed of both Republicans and conservative Democrats. (261)

6.69. At the second reading stage, after Texas House floor debate on a bill has ended and any amendments have been approved, a vote is taken on passage to _____. (267)

6.70. After a bill has passed in the Texas House and Senate, it may be killed by a gubernatorial _____. (269)

6.71. The attorney general of Texas has an opportunity to influence legislation when asked to issue an _____ on the constitutionality of a bill. (271)

6.72. Authorizing special research projects by its staff is one of the functions of the Texas Legislative _____. (273)

6.73. In addition to conducting research in diverse areas, the Texas Senate Research Center performs the bill _____ function. (274)

F. Completion Questions on Readings (with textbook page numbers)

6.74. Following redistricting in 2001, the Texas House elected a Republican speaker in 2003 for the first time since the end of the _____ era. (282)

6.75. Bipartisan redistricting cooperation in California in 2001 has been attributed to "a mutual fear of the unknown" that produced an example of "_____ politics." (283)

6.76. Representative Ron Wilson wants to turn the Houston Astrodome into a state _____. (285)

6.77. Representative Harvey Hildebran attributes Representative Ron Wilson's abilities to his membership on the leadership _____ of three House speakers. (287)

6.78. Sponsorship levels for the Texas Public Policy Foundation's "Legislative Policy Orientation for 2003" were named after U.S. _____. (288)

6.79. A fund-raising letter soliciting lobbyists' financial support for the TPPF's "Legislative Policy Orientation for 2003" listed the name of each lobbyist's top _____. (289)

G.   Essay Questions (with textbook page numbers)

1. Write an essay entitled "Constitutional Provisions Concerning Regular and Special Sessions of the Texas Legislature." Include criticisms of these provisions, and explain why you recommend making changes or maintaining the current arrangement. (234)
2. Write an essay entitled "Redistricting the Texas Legislature at the Beginning of the Twenty-first Century." (235-239)
3. Assume that you are briefing a group of students who will be visiting the Texas House and Senate for the first time. What will you tell them concerning constitutional requirements for House and Senate members and concerning characteristics of the membership of each chamber? (243-249)
4. Outline the principal powers and immunities of members of the Texas Legislature, and explain why you believe these powers and immunities should be retained, increased, decreased, or abolished. (250-253)
5. Describe the principal powers of the president of the Texas Senate. (254-255)
6. List the principal powers of the speaker of the Texas House of Representatives, and describe the process whereby the speaker is elected. (255-257)
7. Describe the committee systems of the Texas House and Senate. Then suggest possible reforms or explain why you believe the systems should remain unchanged. (257-259)
8. Identify the major caucuses that have been established in the Texas Legislature. Then explain why these caucuses have been organized, and comment on their effectiveness. (259-261)

9. Outline and briefly describe the procedural steps beginning with introduction of a bill in the Texas House of Representatives and ending with possible actions by the governor after passage by both the House and the Senate. (262-270)

10. Identify the principal sources of influence in the legislative environment, and explain why you believe that these influences are or are not conducive to effective policymaking by the Texas Legislature. (270-275)

11. In bicameral legislatures, the Senate always has fewer members than the other chamber. Using data in the How Do We Compare Box at the bottom of page 233 of this chapter, determine the ratio of Senate seats to House or Assembly seats in each state. Calculate this ratio to the nearest tenth by dividing the number of House or Assembly seats by the number of Senate seats. For example, the ratio for Texas is 1 to 4.8. To compare Texas with other states, rank the 8 states with bicameral legislatures in descending order of their Senate to House ratios.

12. Using data in the How Do We Compare Box at the top of page 241 of this chapter, rank the states in descending order according to annual salaries for their legislators. Does this ranking suggest that salaries of Texas legislators should be raised or that salaries in other states should be lowered? What factors should be considered in determining the compensation of legislators?

13. Using data in the How Do We Compare box at the top of page 251 of this chapter, determine the ratio of bills passed to bills introduced in 2000–2001. For example, the ratio for the Texas Legislature was 1 to 3.5. This ratio is obtained by dividing the number of bills introduced by the number of bills passed. For a clearer picture of how the Texas Legislature compares, rank the eight states in descending order of their ratios.

III. *Applying Your Knowledge*

A. Outside Readings and Cartoons

1. From the endnotes for this chapter or from the updated bibliography of selected sources accessible through the Houghton Mifflin Political Science home page (politcalscience.college.hmco.com), choose a magazine article or a journal article and write a summary of it.

2. From the endnotes for this chapter or from the updated bibliography of selected sources accessible through the Houghton Mifflin Political Science home page (politicalscience.college.hmco.com), choose a book and write a summary of one of its chapters.

3. Find a newspaper editorial that relates to the Texas Legislature. Summarize that editorial, and explain why you agree or disagree with the writer's point of view.

4. Find a newspaper article concerning the Texas Legislature. Summarize the article, and describe what you do and/or do not like about that piece of reporting.

5. Interpret one of this chapter's cartoons (or another cartoon concerning the legislature), and explain why you agree or disagree with the cartoonist's point of view.

6. Explore two or more of the web sites listed among sources for this chapter. Then select one site and write a brief note outlining how its information contributes to your understanding of the Texas Legislature.

B. Internet Research Project

Objectives

1. To explain some functions of the Texas Legislative Council.
2. To familiarize students with the identity of their state representatives and state senators.
3. To inform students of the committee assignments of their state representatives and senators.
4. To enhance students' awareness of some of the characteristics of their state representative districts.
5. To enhance student understanding of FAQs on web sites.

URL. http://www.capitol.state.tx.us

Description of the Site. The Texas Legislative Council maintains this site, entitled *Texas Legislature Online.* Functions of the council include assisting the legislature in drafting proposed legislation; revising existing legislation to organize and clarify statutes; investigating departments, agencies, state officials, and other matters as the legislature may request; and providing information technology support to several legislative agencies. The site is linked to web sites maintained by the Texas Senate, the Texas House of Representatives, and other state agencies and offices. In addition, *Texas Legislature Online* provides texts of the Texas Constitution and state statutes, information about individual bills (including bill text, fiscal notes, bill analyses, author, caption, and legislative actions), and committee schedules.

General information about Texas's legislative process is also available, including a legislative glossary and a discussion of how a bill becomes a law. Also included is a web page for frequently asked questions (FAQs) about the site. Either directly or through the FAQs, citizens are able to identify the legislators who represent them.

The internet is a dynamic, ever-changing environment. If any of the links and instructions need to be adjusted, consult the textbook website for updates of this exercise (http://college.hmco.com/polisci/brown/prac_tex_pol/12e/students/index.html).

Use of Information. Based on data obtained from "Texas Legislature Online" you will be able to answer questions about your state senator and state representative.

1. Go to "Texas Legislature Online" (www.capitol.state.tx.us) and click on the hypertext "Who Represents Me?" This will take you to the "Find Your Incumbent" page.

2. Click on the hyperlink entitled "By Address."

3. Enter your street address and zip code.

4. Click on "Submit." Then click on "Display District Information."

5. You should now have the names and district numbers of your U.S. representative, state senator, state representative, and member of the Texas State Board of Education. For this exercise, you are only interested in your state senator and state representative.

6. What is the name and the district number of your Texas state senator?

   _____

7. What is the name and the district number of your Texas state representative?

   _____

8. Each chamber of the legislature sponsors its own web site, which includes information about each representative or senator, including committee assignments.

9. On your senator's web page, scroll down to "Committee Membership" and list the committees to which your senator has been appointed.

   _____

   _____

10. Back up one page and click on your state representative's hyperlink and scroll down to. "Committee Assignment." To what House committees has your representative been appointed?

    _____

    _____

11. On your representative's page, locate the section labeled "Research." Click on "Bills." Once there, locate the section labeled "Bills by Author."
    a. Click on the most recent regular session (not special session) of the legislature.
    b. Under "Bill by Author," click on your representative's name.
    c. How many bills were authored by your representative during the most recent regular session? _____

12. Another way to reach the FYI page is through the "Frequently Asked Questions" page. Go to the *Texas Legislature Online* home page (http://www.capitol.tx.us) and click on "Help." Then go to the question, "How do I determine my district and legislator?" Click here; the answer to this question will include a hyperlink to the web page "Find Your Incumbent (FYI)".

Internet Research Tip. Web sites often have a page devoted to frequently asked questions, identified as FAQs. This section provides information about the site and anticipates questions a new user might have. You will find FAQs helpful in navigating a site with which you are unfamiliar. *Texas Legislature Online's* FAQs are typical of FAQ pages on other sites. Note that the page includes information on site availability, frequency of updates, how to download data, and how to obtain specific material related to the legislature (such as how to communicate with legislators, how to follow the status of a bill, and how to find out how a legislator voted on specific bills). It is advisable to review FAQs in your preliminary research.

Answers

True-False: Text	Multiple-Choice: Text	Completion: Text
6.1. T	6.30. a	6.56. odd
6.2. T	6.31. d	6.57. odd
6.3. F	6.32. c	6.58. gerrymandering
6.4. T	6.33. b	6.59. lower
6.5. T	6.34. c	6.60. 26
6.6. F	6.35. b	6.61. Jordan
6.7. F	6.36. b	6.62. suburban
6.8. T	6.37. b	6.63. continuance
6.9. T	6.38. d	6.64. simple
6.10. T	6.39. b	6.65. bracket
6.11. F	6.40. b	6.66. subpoena
6.12. T	6.41. c	6.67. margarita
6.13. F	6.42. b	6.68. Conservative
6.14. F	6.43. d	6.69. engrossment
6.15. T	6.44. c	6.70. veto
6.16. F	6.45. b	6.71. opinion
6.17. T	6.46. d	6.72. Council
6.18. F	6.47. d	6.73. analysis
6.19. F	6.48. a	
6.20. T	6.49. c	Completion: Readings
6.21. F		
6.22. F	Multiple-Choice: Readings	6.74. Reconstruction
6.23. T		6.75. hedge
	6.50. d	6.76. casino
True-False: Readings	6.51. c	6.77. teams
	6.52. a	6.78. presidents
6.24. F	6.53. a	6.79. client
6.25. F	6.54. a	
6.26. F	6.55. c	
6.27. T		
6.28. F		
6.29. F		

CHAPTER SEVEN

The Executive

I. *Preparing to Study*

A. Performance Objectives

After studying and reviewing the text and readings in this chapter, you will be able to:

1. Describe the Texas executive structure as outlined in a flow chart showing the governor, department heads, and important boards and commissions.
2. Explain the importance of money in gubernatorial politics.
3. Identify state constitutional provisions concerning the qualifications, term of office, and compensation of the governor of Texas.
4. Identify state constitutional provisions concerning gubernatorial succession and the process of impeaching and removing a Texas governor.
5. Explain the functions and importance of the governor's staff.
6. Outline the principal executive powers of the governor.
7. Outline the principal legislative powers of the governor.
8. Outline the principal judicial powers of the governor.
9. Describe some informal powers of the governor.
10. Describe the principal powers and functions of the appointed secretary of state and the popularly elected heads of executive departments.

B. Overview of the Text (pp. 293–319)

The governor is the most visible figure in Texas state government. Although commonly called the "chief executive," the governor shares power with other elected officials.

Looking Back (pp. 293–294). A "weak-executive" pattern of organization is provided in the Constitution of 1876 to prevent gubernatorial domination, like that exercised by Governor E. J. Davis, Jr., during the Reconstruction era following the Civil War.

Overview of the Governorship (pp. 295–302)

Although the Texas Constitution does not establish financial qualifications for the office of governor, it is a fact that serious gubernatorial candidates and recent governors have been wealthy or have had significant financial support from rich individuals and well-financed special interest groups. The Texas Constitution does specify that the governor must be at least 30 years old, a U.S. citizen, and a resident of Texas for a minimum of five years immediately preceding election. Like other elected executive officials, the governor is elected for a four-year term. Removal can be accomplished by impeachment in the House and conviction in the Senate. Less than 200 state employees serve as staff members within the Governor's Office.

Powers of the Governor (pp. 303–311).

The constitutional powers of the governor include appointment of most members of state boards and commissions, with confirmation by a two-thirds majority vote of the Senate. Independent gubernatorial removal power is limited to members of the governor's staff and some statutory officials. Although the governor proposes a state budget, the legislature pays more attention to the budget produced by its own Legislative Budget Board. Nevertheless, the governor can veto a whole appropriations bill or specific budget items.

Executive orders are used to set policy within the executive branch and to create or abolish various study and advisory bodies. Proclamations are used for ceremonial purposes as well as for other matters, such as calling special elections and declaring a region to be a disaster area.

Legislative affairs are influenced by the governor's vetoes, messages to the legislature, and calls for special legislative sessions. In judicial matters, gubernatorial influence is exerted through appointment of judges to district and appellate courts when vacancies occur between elections. The governor is also involved in administering justice by granting pardons, reprieves, and commutations of sentences. The Board of Pardons and Paroles, however, must recommend most such actions. Informal powers are exercised through the governor's participation in public ceremonies and press interviews.

The Plural Executive (pp. 311–318).

First in line of succession in the event of death, resignation, or removal of the governor is the lieutenant governor, who also serves as president of the Senate. The attorney general is the state's principal legal officer and is responsible for issuing opinions on legal questions raised by state and local officials.

The commissioner of the General Land Office administers the vast lands owned by the state—lands that produce many millions of dollars of annual revenue from rents and mineral leases. The Department of Agriculture is headed by the commissioner of agriculture, who directs services designed to aid farmers and ranchers and is responsible for enforcing regulatory statutes affecting agriculture.

The comptroller of public accounts is the state's principal tax collector and custo-
dian of state funds. In addition, the comptroller selects the banks that serve as de-
positories for the state's money.

Unlike the aforementioned elected officials, the secretary of state is appointed
by the governor. This executive officer performs diverse tasks that include issuing
charters for corporations, supervising the administration of Texas election laws, and
(unofficially but traditionally) serving as the governor's adviser and assistant in political matters.

Looking Ahead (pp. 318–319). Constitutional changes in the power and structure
of the governor's office and the offices of other elected executive officials would
require one or more constitutional amendments or a new state constitution. A proposed constitutional revision resolution submitted by Senator Bill Ratliff and Representative Rob Junnell in 1999, for example, would provide a cabinet structure for
the executive branch. Neither the legislature, nor Governor George W. Bush, nor
Governor Rick Perry showed interest in this proposal. Without change, the state
will continue with a constitutionally weak governor who has limited influence over
much of the executive branch.

C. **Key Terms** (with textbook page numbers)

Governor's Office (302)
appointive power (303)
recess appointment (304)
removal power (304)
martial law (305)
law enforcement power (305)
budgetary power (306)
executive order (306)
proclamation (307)
legislative power (307)
message power (308)
veto power (308)
item veto (308)
postadjournment veto (308)

parole (310)
executive clemency (310)
full pardon (310)
conditional pardon (310)
reprieve (310)
commutation of sentence (310)
plural executive (311)
lieutenant governor (312)
attorney general (313)
comptroller of public accounts (315)
commissioner of the General Land Office (316)
commissioner of agriculture (317)
secretary of state (318)

D.   Overview of the Readings (pp. 322–331)

7.1.   "Firms Help Pay the Tab" by George Kuempel (pp. 322–323)

Austin's 2003 inauguration celebration for Governor Rick Perry and Lieutenant
Governor David Dewhurst included a giant barbecue, a big-time ball, a long parade,
and other events attended by thousands Texans. While most celebrants bought
modestly priced tickets for the barbecue and ball, some paid much more. Corporate
donors gave as much as $50,000. Citizen watchdog groups questioned what extras
these donors, many with an interest in bills up for consideration by the 78th Legislature, got for their money. Corporate officials and lobbyists denied any ulterior mo-
tives, saying that they were simply good citizens helping to offset some of the inaugural costs in order to make tickets cheaper and more accessible to Texans.

7.2.   "Executive Order Creating the Governor's Clean Coal Technology Council" by
Governor Rick Perry (pp. 324–326)

Texas governors have power to issue orders that set policy within the executive
branch and create entities such as councils, task forces, and boards. Governor Rick
Perry's Executive Order RP21 creates the Governor's Clean Coal Technology
Council. The document's preamble explains the importance of coal as a source of
energy as well as the need for good air quality. The body of the order concerns the
council's duties, membership, and operations. Unlike a law, an executive order is
made under the governor's exclusive authority and remains in effect until modified,
amended, rescinded, or superceded by the issuing governor or a subsequent governor.

7.3.   "Excerpts from Governor Rick Perry's State of the State Address, 13 February
2003" by Governor Rick Perry (pp. 326–331)

Texas governors use their State of the State Address to highlight achievements, explain broad goals, and lay out an agenda for a regular legislative session. Rick
Perry's 2003 address did just this. Noting the creation of new jobs in Houston and
San Antonio, he also discussed the achievements of Texas school children. Perry
then made clear his priorities: education, security, and, especially, reduced state
spending. Further, he explained his rationale for selecting these priorities. Finally,
the governor outlined particular legislative initiatives, especially those related to his
goals for the 78th regular session. The State of the State address gave Governor
Perry a chance to speak directly to members of the 78th Legislature, as well as to
communicate with other Texans, and to seek support for his policy agenda.

II.   *Testing Your Knowledge*

A.   **True-False Questions on Text Material** (with textbook page numbers)

_____ 7.1. During the Reconstruction era, Texas's strong executive government earned the confidence and support of most of the state's citizens. (293)

_____ 7.2. The Texas state government operates without a genuine chief executive officer. (295)

_____ 7.3. The minimum age for a Texas governor is 35 years. (297)

_____ 7.4. After election in 1978, Bill Clements became Texas's first Republican governor since E. J. Davis held that office. (297)

_____ 7.5. Richard Coke was serving as governor of Texas when the Constitution of 1876 was written. (298)

_____ 7.6. Under Texas law, a governor is not allowed to hold another civil or corporate office. (300)

_____ 7.7. The Texas Constitution specifies that a mentally incapacitated governor will be suspended from that office and replaced by the lieutenant governor. (300)

_____ 7.8. Under provisions of the Texas Constitution, a governor who is impeached and removed from office may not be tried subsequently in any civil or criminal proceeding. (301)

_____ 7.9. The Texas Constitution specifies several prohibited acts that may result in impeachment and removal of a governor. (302)

_____ 7.10. The governor's personal staff functions directly under gubernatorial supervision. (302)

_____ 7.11. A regular gubernatorial term begins in November of the even-numbered year before a presidential election. (303)

_____ 7.12. The practical politics of senatorial courtesy requires that the governor consult with a prospective appointee's state senator before sending the name to the Senate for confirmation. (304)

_____ 7.13. Under certain circumstances, the governor may assume command of the Texas Rangers. (305)

_____ 7.14. At the commencement of each regular session of the legislature, the governor of Texas is required by the State Constitution to deliver a "State of the State" address. (307)

_____ 7.15. The Texas Legislature frequently overrides vetoes by the governor. (308)

_____ 7.16. The lieutenant governor serves as speaker of the Texas House of Representatives. (312)

_____ 7.17. Unless an appropriations bill is enacted by a four-fifths majority vote in both houses of the Texas Legislature, the comptroller of public accounts must certify that revenue is expected to be available to cover all proposed expenditures. (315)

_____ 7.18. Because the Texas Constitution prohibits depositing any of the state's money in nongovernmental institutions, the comptroller of public accounts must keep all state funds in a special vault located in the basement of the Capitol. (315)

B.   True-False Questions on Readings (with textbook page numbers)

_____ 7.19. Appropriated public funds covered most of the cost of inaugural activities in January 2003. (323)

_____ 7.20. Executive directors for Public Citizen and Common Cause of Texas approved private and corporate financing of inaugural festivities honoring Governor Rick Perry and Lieutenant Governor David Dewhurst in 2003. (323)

_____ 7.21. The Governor's Clean Coal Technology Council is responsible for identifying cleaner coal-fired electric generation technologies. (325)

_____ 7.22. The executive order creating the Governor's Clean Coal Technology Council remains in effect until modified, amended, rescinded, or superseded by Governor Rick Perry or by a succeeding governor. (325)

_____ 7.23. Concerning higher education, Governor Rick Perry in his 2003 inaugural address said that he was joining Speaker Tom Craddick in calling for free tuition for all Texas residents at community colleges and state universities.

_____ 7.24. In his 2003 inaugural address, Governor Rick Perry called for a 9 percent increase in state spending. (328)

C. Multiple-Choice Questions on Text Material (with textbook page numbers)

_____ 7.25. Who among the following meets the constitutional qualifications for the office of governor of Texas? (297)

    a. An alien, age 35, who has been a legal resident of the state for 10 years immediately before the gubernatorial election.

    b. A naturalized U.S. citizen, age 28, who has been a resident of Texas for three years immediately before the gubernatorial election.

    c. A U.S. citizen, age 30, who has resided in Texas for 5 years immediately before the gubernatorial election.

    d. A U.S. citizen born in Texas, age 40, who resided in New Mexico until moving to Texas 60 days before the gubernatorial election.

_____ 7.26. For the second time in the twentieth century, the Texas gubernatorial election campaign of 1996 resulted in the election of (297)

    a. a Republican governor.

    b. a woman governor.

    c. a Libertarian governor.

    d. an African-American governor.

_____ 7.27. A Texas governor is removed from office after impeachment by (301)

    a. the Senate and conviction by the House.

    b. the House and conviction by the Supreme Court of Texas.

    c. the Senate and conviction by the Court of Criminal Appeals.

    d. the House and conviction by the Senate.

_____ 7.28. The Texas governor who was impeached and removed from office was (301)

    a. Miriam A. Ferguson.

    b. James E. Ferguson.

    c. Preston Smith.

    d. John Connally.

_____ 7.29. The principal reason for the growth of the Texas governor's staff has been (302)

    a. the state taxing and spending programs.

    b. the legislative activities of the House and Senate.

    c. the chief executive's activist approach to statewide issues.

    d. the need for local and state law enforcement programs.

7.30. In recent years, the Governor's Office in Texas has been greatly influenced by the increasing importance of (302)

   a. intergovernmental relations.
   b. interstate commerce.
   c. private educational institutions from kindergartens to universities.
   d. national security.

7.31. The governor's appointive power is classified as (303)

   a. an executive power.
   b. a legislative power.
   c. a judicial power.
   d. an informal power.

7.32. The governor of Texas appoints the (303)

   a. secretary of state.
   b. commissioner of agriculture.
   c. comptroller of public accounts.
   d. members of the Texas Railroad Commission.

7.33. According to the Texas Constitution, the governor must call a special election to fill a vacancy in Texas's (304)

   a. Railroad Commission.
   b. House of Representatives.
   c. Supreme Court.
   d. Court of Criminal Appeals.

7.34. The Texas governor's independent removal power extends to members of (305)

   a. all state boards and state commissions.
   b. all state boards but not state commissions.
   c. all state commissions but not state boards.
   d. the governor's staff.

7.35. Acting alone, the governor of Texas may (306)

   a. impound funds appropriated by the legislature.
   b. veto an individual budget item in an appropriations bill.
   c. transfer funds from one state agency to another.
   d. increase or decrease an appropriation.

_____ 7.36. By custom, the governor of Texas delivers a farewell address to the legislature (307)

    a. at the end of each regular legislative session.
    b. before leaving the state on official business.
    c. at the conclusion of a gubernatorial term of office.
    d. at the end of each calendar year.

_____ 7.37. Under the Texas Constitution, the governor has power to (309)

    a. introduce bills and resolutions in both chambers of the legislature.
    b. appoint the lieutenant governor.
    c. remove state senators and representatives.
    d. call special sessions of the legislature.

_____ 7.38. The governor of Texas plays the role of chief of state when (311)

    a. vetoing a bill.
    b. appointing a judge.
    c. participating in the dedication of a new state building.
    d. granting a pardon.

_____ 7.39. Under Texas law, opinions issued by the attorney general are authoritative unless overruled by a new law or the ruling of (314)

    a. the governor.
    b. a court.
    c. the comptroller of public accounts.
    d. the State Bar of Texas.

_____ 7.40. The commissioner of the General Land Office oversees the growth and development of the state's (316)

    a. Highway Trust Fund.
    b. Permanent School Fund.
    c. General Revenue Fund.
    d. Teacher Retirement Fund.

_____ 7.41. The secretary of state is charged with (318)

    a. tabulating election returns for state and district offices.
    b. collecting most state taxes.
    c. serving as the governor's legal counsel.
    d. auditing financial records of all elected state officials.

D.   **Multiple-Choice Questions on Readings** (with textbook page numbers)

_____   7.42.   Concerning his company's donation of $50,000 for the 2003 inaugura-
tion festivities in Austin, AT&T's vice president for governmental affairs stated that his company expected (323)

a.   no benefit.
b.   preferential treatment by the legislature.
c.   preferential treatment by the governor.
d.   preferential treatment by the Supreme Court of Texas.

_____   7.43.   Consumer advocates Tom "Smitty" Smith and Suzy Woodford want to
eliminate the question of whether inaugural donors buy access to government officials by (323)

a.   using public money to pay all expenses.
b.   ending inaugural galas.
c.   using campaign funds to pay all expenses.
d.   raising ticket prices.

_____   7.44.   Governor Rick Perry's Executive Order RP21 states that coal is important to Texans because it (324)

a.   is more plentiful than petroleum.
b.   is an especially clean-burning fuel.
c.   provides employment for millions of Texans.
d.   helps keep electricity prices low in Texas.

_____   7.45.   Included among the duties of the Governor's Clean Coal Technology
Council is advising the governor concerning the feasibility of developing clean coal technologies in Texas to (325)

a.   replace all other sources of electric power.
b.   reduce emissions from existing coal-fired electric generation.
c.   free Texas from the need to import fuels from other states and
countries.
d.   boost Texas's lignite industry.

_____   7.46.   In his 2003 inaugural address, Governor Perry included among his top
three priorities (327-328)

a.   congressional redistricting.
b.   highway construction.
c.   education.
d.   environmental protection.

_____ 7.47. In his 2003 inaugural address, Governor Perry asserted that the state budget could be balanced *without* (329)

    a. changing the point of collection for the gas tax.
    b. raising taxes.
    c. eliminating state boards.
    d. eliminating state commissions.

E.   Completion Questions on Text Material (with textbook page numbers)

7.48. Governor Ann Richards appointed record numbers of Latinos, African Americans, and _____ to high office. (298)

7.49. Early in his political career, Rick Perry was elected for three terms in the Texas House of Representatives as a _____ Party candidate. (299)

7.50. The annual salary of the governor of Texas is determined by the _____. (300)

7.51. In Texas, impeachment proceedings are highly charged political affairs with _____ overtones. (302)

7.52. When assuming office, the governor of Texas takes an oath "to cause the laws to be faithfully _____." (303)

7.53. A gubernatorial appointment made while the Texas Legislature is not in session is called a _____ appointment. (304)

7.54. The governor makes an interim appointment to fill the vacancy when a U.S. _____ from Texas dies or resigns before the expiration of a term. (304)

7.55. If deemed necessary because of civil disorder, the governor of Texas may declare _____ law and suspend civil authority. (305)

7.56. The Texas governor may exercise control over state spending by vetoing an entire _____ bill. (306)

7.57. The governor of Texas may exercise a postadjournment veto by rejecting any pending legislation within _____ days after the end of a legislative session. (308)

7.58. More than half of Texas's judges who serve on district or appellate courts originally obtain those offices as a result of appointment by the _____. (309)

7.59. With more than one independently elected official, Texas' state executive structure is referred to collectively as the _____ executive. (311)

7.60. Texas's lieutenant governor functions more in the _____ area than in
the executive branch. (312)

7.61. The annual salary of Texas's lieutenant governor is $_____. (312)

7.62. The Texas attorney general serves as the state's chief _____. (314)

7.63. The comptroller of public accounts is Texas's chief accounting officer and
_____ collector. (315)

7.64. Beginning a second term in January 2003, Comptroller Carole Keeton Strayhorn
is the self-styled "tough _____" of Texas state politics. (316)

7.65. Powers of Texas's commissioner of the General Land Office include awarding oil,
gas, and sulfur exploration _____ for land owned by the state. (316)

7.66. One of the duties of the Texas commissioner of agriculture is to control the use of
_____. (317)

7.67. Granting _____ to Texas corporations is a duty of the state's secretary of state. (318)

F.   Completion Questions on Readings (with textbook page numbers)

7.68. According to Tom "Smitty" Smith, executive director of Public Citizen, corporations don't contribute money to pay for inaugural celebrations "if they are not get-
ting a _____ on their investment." (322)

7.69. Based on ticket sales, the 2003 inaugural ball at the Austin Convention Center
attracted _____ participants. (323)

7.70. The Governor's Clean Coal Technology Council is charged with advising the
governor on the potential of clean coal technologies to _____ the efficiency of coal-fired electric generation. (325)

7.71. The chair and vice chair of the Governor's Clean Coal Technology Council are
appointed by the _____. (325)

7.72. In his 2003 inaugural address, Governor Perry stated that half a million children
are covered under the Children's _____ Insurance Program. (326)

7.73. In his 2003 inaugural address, Governor Perry explained that the state's job base
will expand by thousands because _____ is coming to San Antonio. (326)

G. Essay Questions (with textbook page numbers)

1. Write an essay on "The Political Significance of the 2003 Inaugural Ceremony and Festivities Honoring Governor Rick Perry and Lieutenant Governor David Dewhurst." (295–297)
2. Write an overview of the office of governor of Texas in which you comment on qualifications for the office, term of office, compensation, succession, and method of removal. (297–302)
3. Write an essay on "Appointment and Removal Powers of the Governor of Texas." (303–305)
4. Write an essay on "Budgetary Powers of the Governor of Texas." (306)
5. Write an essay on "Legislative Powers of the Governor of Texas." (307–309)
6. Write an essay on "Judicial Powers of the Governor of Texas." (309–310)
7. Describe the principal powers and functions of Texas's secretary of state and the following state executive officials who are elected by Texas voters: lieutenant governor, attorney general, commissioner of the General Land Office, commissioner of agriculture, and comptroller of public accounts. (311–318)
8. Using data in the How Do We Compare box at the top of page 300 of this chapter, rank the eight states in descending order according to the amount of each governor's salary. How does Texas compare? Do these data suggest that the salaries of governors compare favorably with the salaries of head football coaches and presidents at state universities?
9. Using data in the How Do We Compare box at the top of page 300 of this chapter, rank the eight states according to the number of people working in the governor's office. How does Texas compare? Keep in mind the fact that these data do not reflect "off-budget" personnel who may work for the governor but are paid by an outside source, such as a political party.

III. Applying Your Knowledge

A. Outside Readings and Cartoons

1. From the endnotes for this chapter or from the updated bibliography of selected sources accessible through the Houghton Mifflin Political Science home page (politcalscience.college.hmco.com), choose a magazine or journal article and write a summary of it.
2. From the endnotes for this chapter or from the updated bibliography of selected sources available through the Houghton Mifflin Political Science home page (politicalscience.college.hmco.com), choose a book and write a summary of one of its chapters.

3. In a newspaper, find an editorial that relates to the governor, lieutenant governor, or an elected head of a department of the executive branch of Texas state government. Summarize that editorial, and explain why you agree or disagree with the writer's point of view.

4. Find a newspaper article concerning the governor, lieutenant governor, or an elected head of a department of the executive branch of Texas state government. Summarize that article, and describe what you do and/or do not like about this piece of reporting.

5. Interpret one of this chapter's cartoons (or another cartoon relating to the executive branch), and explain why you agree or disagree with the cartoonist's point of view.

6. Explore two or more of the web sites listed among sources for this chapter. Then select one site and write a brief note outlining how its information contributes to your understanding of the executive branch of Texas state government.

B. Internet Research Project

Objectives

1. To enhance student understanding of the functions of the governor's office.
2. To familiarize students with the procedure for obtaining a commission or board appointment.
3. To increase student awareness of the importance of senatorial courtesy in obtaining a gubernatorial appointment.
4. To expose students to the use of the "Back" and "Forward" icons.

URL. http://www.governor.state.tx.us

Description of the Site. The Office of the Governor maintains this site. It includes press releases about the governor, a description of initiatives (or issues) that are important to the governor, and a description of the functions of the Governor's Office. Hyperlinks are provided to Texas' strategic plan (developed by the Governor's Office), state and federal grant opportunities, and available board and commission appointments.

One of the most important powers of the governor is the ability to nominate individuals to serve on boards and commissions. A list of available positions is maintained on the site, including the affected boards or commissions, the number of openings for each, and the date by which each position will become available. Further information can be obtained from the Appointments Division by mail or fax.

The Internet is a dynamic, ever-changing environment. If any of the links and instructions need to be adjusted, consult the textbook web site for updates of this exercise (http://college.hmco.com/polisci/brown/prac_tex_pol/12e/students/index.html).

Use of Information. Assume that the governor has contacted you and advised you that there are a number of board and commission positions available. Because you have been such a loyal supporter of the governor over the years, you may select the appointment you would like.

1. First you will need to go to the governor's web site (http://www.governor.state.tx.us).

2. Locate the "Quick Links" section on the page. Click on the "Appointments" hyperlink. Then click on "Eligible Appointments List." Review the available appointments and select the agency, commission, or department to which you would like to be nominated.

3. What agency did you select?

    _____

4. How many appointments are/will be available at the agency?

    _____

5. When do/did the position(s) become available?

    _____

6. Back up to the Appointments page. Click on the "List of Appointments" hyperlink. What agency has the largest number of appointments? How many positions? _____

7. To obtain more information about the agency you selected in #3, go to the following web site for the Texas State Library and Archives (http://www2.tsl.state.tx.us/trail/agencies.jsp). This site includes an alphabetical listing of all state agencies, departments, and commissions. The Texas Records and Information Locator (TRAIL), maintained by the Texas State Library, includes budgetary, regulatory, and statutory information about some departments. This site contains links to generic information about the agency (TRAIL Page), the agency's web page (if the agency has created one), and online publications of the agency.

    If your first choice cannot be found on this list, select an agency that is in the index and has a web site. Click on the agency's "TRAIL page" and review its generic site.

8. Click on the hyperlink to the agency's website, if it maintains its own site, to review more information about the agency. If your first choice does not maintain a separate site, select an agency that does have one. Since each agency has its own formatting method, you will need to navigate through the site following the hyperlink prompts.

9. What are the functions or responsibilities of the agency?

_____

Once the governor has nominated you for a board, agency, or commission, the Texas Senate will have to approve the appointment at the next legislative session. Senate approval is required whether the legislature is in special session or in regular session. Unless your state senator agrees to your appointment, it is unlikely you will be approved because of the practice of senatorial courtesy. It will therefore be necessary for you to confer with your state senator to assure support for your nomination.

10. Return to the FYI (Find Your Incumbent) site discussed in Chapter 6 of this *Study Guide* and follow the directions to obtain the name of your state senator.

11. What is the name of your state senator?

_____

Internet Research Tip. You have been required to refer to different web pages within the web site to complete this exercise. You can use your web browser, the software program you use to view the web pages, to move quickly among the pages within the web site. At the top of the page are icons for the "Back," "Forward," "Home," "Reload," and "Stop" functions. Use the "Back" and "Forward" icons to move among previously accessed pages. To return to the first site chosen, click on the "Home" icon. If the web browser is having trouble connecting with a site, use the "Reload" icon to begin the transmission again. To terminate the transmission of information from a web site, click on the "Stop" icon.

Answers

True-False: Text	Multiple-Choice: Text	Completion: Text
7.1. F	7.25. c	7.48. Women
7.2. T	7.26. a	7.49. Democratic
7.3. F	7.27. d	7.50. legislature
7.4. T	7.28. b	7.51. legal
7.5. T	7.29. c	7.52. executed
7.6. T	7.30. a	7.53. recess
7.7. F	7.31. a	7.54. senator
7.8. F	7.32. a	7.55. martial
7.9. F	7.33. b	7.56. appropriations
7.10. T	7.34. d	7.57. 20
7.11. F	7.35. b	7.58. governor
7.12. T	7.36. c	7.59. plural
7.13. T	7.37. d	7.60. legislative
7.14. T	7.38. c	7.61. 7,200
7.15. F	7.39. b	7.62. lawyer
7.16. F	7.40. b	7.63. tax
7.17. T	7.41. a	7.64. grandma
7.18. F		7.65. leases
		7.66. pesticides

True-False: Readings	Multiple-Choice: Readings	7.67. charters
7.19. F	7.42. a	
7.20. F	7.43. a	Completion: Readings
7.21. T	7.44. d	
7.22. T	7.45. b	7.68. return
7.23. F	7.46. c	7.69. 10,000
7.24. F	7.47. b	7.70. increase
		7.71. governor
		7.72. Health
		7.73. Toyota

CHAPTER EIGHT

Public Policy and Administration

I. *Preparing to Study*

A. Performance Objectives

After studying and reviewing the text and readings in this chapter, you will be able to:

1. Describe the size of the state bureaucracy, compensation for state employees, problems involving representation of women and minorities in top management positions, and the means whereby citizens receive customer service in coping with bureaucratic problems.
2. Describe the organization and responsibilities of the State Board of Education (SBOE), and discuss current problems and programs in public education from kindergarten through high school.
3. Describe Texas' system of higher education—public community and junior colleges, state universities, and state technical colleges—and discuss important issues relating to organization, direction, and funding.
4. Describe the organization and function of state agencies providing social services; and comment on the need for government intervention to provide some Texans with temporary financial assistance, health and mental health care, and help in finding employment.
5. Explain the implementation of economic policies by state agencies in the areas of business regulation and promotion.
6. Identify Texas's important environmental problems and describe the work of state agencies that are responsible for dealing with these problems.
7. Explain the sunset process for coping with the problem of bureaucratic proliferation in Texas government.

B. Overview of the Text (pp. 333–364)

In any organization, people who do the work determine its success or failure. This chapter concerns government personnel as well as the organization and function of various state agencies. Of particular importance is the role of the governor in appointing members of the boards and commissions that head most of these agencies.

Overview of Public Policy and Administration (333). The Texas bureaucracy consists of the employees who do the administrative work of state government. This chapter focuses on five areas of public policy and administration: education, social services, economic regulation, environmental protection, and homeland security.

State Employees (pp. 334–337). Counting both full-time and part-time employees, about 335,000 Texans held state jobs in 2003. This amounted to a full-time equivalent total of 282,000 employed by state agencies and by state colleges and universities. Texas does not have a central personnel office. Each agency determines its own personnel policies; but the legislature sets the pay scale for state service and regulates holidays, vacation time, and days of sick leave. Some personnel reductions have resulted from efforts to balance the state budget without raising taxes. Through use of a toll-free number, complaints against state agencies and their personnel may be directed to the governor's office.

Education (pp. 337–348). Headed by a commissioner appointed by the governor, the Texas Education Agency (TEA) has headquarters in Austin. Teachers, administrators, and other employees in Texas's more than 1,000 independent school districts staff public schools for young Texans at all levels from kindergarten through high school. Overseeing TEA is the State Board of Education (SBOE), which is composed of 15 members elected from single-member districts. Controversies over the SBOE's role in rejecting textbooks and placing textbooks on "conforming" or "nonconforming" lists attract public attention from time to time.

The State Board for Educator Certification (SBEC) regulates the training, certification, and continuing education of public school teachers and administrators. Its 12 voting members are appointed by the governor; the three nonvoting members are appointed by the governor, the commissioner of education, and the commissioner of higher education, respectively.

The Texas Higher Education Coordinating Board provides direction for the efficient and economical operation of the Lone Star State's public community colleges, state universities, and state technical colleges. This board is composed of eighteen members who are appointed by the governor for six-year terms and approved by the Senate. Most of Texas's public universities function as components of six multi-campus university systems that are governed by boards of regents appointed by the governor. The four technical colleges are parts of the Texas State Technical College System. There are 50 community or junior college districts.

Social Services (pp. 348–351). Millions of Texans benefit from social services administered under the direction of the executive commissioner of the Health and Human Services Commission and four commissioners. Each commissioner heads one of four departments: State Health Services, Family and Protective Services, Assistive and Rehabilitative Services, and Aging and Disability Services. Appointed by the governor with the consent of the Senate, the executive commissioner appoints the four commissioners with the consent of the governor. Social services include financial assistance through the Temporary Assistance for Needy Families (TANF) program; medical treatment for people falling below the poverty level through Medicaid; food stamps for the elderly, the disabled, and poor families; mental health facilities to treat mentally ill and mentally retarded people; and job training for unemployed workers.

Economic Policies (pp. 351–357). The popularly elected three-member Railroad Commission is one of the most highly publicized regulatory agencies. Despite its name, the major function of this commission involves regulation of oil and natural gas production. Another important regulatory agency is the Public Utility Commission. It has jurisdiction over rates and services involving telephone companies, electric utilities in unincorporated areas, and radio-telephone service statewide. The Office of Public Utility Counsel has been established to represent consumers in rate cases. Regulation of Texas's insurance industry has been placed in the hands of the commissioner of insurance, who is appointed for a two-year term by the governor with the consent of the Senate. Both the insurance industry and the electric power industry are being deregulated so that competition will play a more important role in meeting the needs of consumers.

Business promotion by the state includes highway construction and maintenance. Headed by a three-member commission appointed by the governor with the consent of the Senate, the Department of Transportation is responsible for the condition of 79,000 miles of Texas highways. Constituting the third largest item in the state budget, highway building and maintenance are critical for meeting important transportation needs of the Texas economy.

Maintaining a state parks system and conserving wildlife are responsibilities of the Texas Parks and Wildlife Commission. Its nine members are appointed by the governor. Both parks (with recreational facilities) and wildlife (fish, birds, and animals) stimulate tourism, which is one of the state's major industries.

People working in many trades and professions (for example, accounting and nursing) are licensed by various state agencies, thus certifying their proficiency and protecting the public. Each licensing board has at least one "public" member who is not employed in the regulated occupation.

Environmental Issues (pp. 358–361). By merging several agencies involved in environmental protection, the Texas Natural Resource Conservation Commission (TNRCC) was created in 1993 to coordinate the state programs for restricting or preventing pollution of Texas's air, water, and soil. At the beginning of September 2002, its name was changed to Texas Commission on Environmental Quality (TCEQ). Appointed by the governor with the consent of the Senate, the three full-time commissioners serve for six-year terms. Although TCEQ has jurisdiction over water pollution, the six-member Texas Water Development Board is responsible for water conservation strategies designed to maximize protection of this critical natural resource. Hazardous waste materials of different kinds (low-level radioactive, high-level radioactive, and nonradioactive) constitute critical environmental and health problems that require government action.

Homeland Security (361–363). Terrorist hijackings of four passenger planes on 11 September 2001 were followed by organization of the Governor's Task Force on Homeland Security. With the task force's recommendations and a growing volume of federal funding, Texas state and local governments have been active in establishing a state health alert network, tightening airport security, assisting hospitals to prepare for dealing with bioterrorism, improving port security, providing food production security on farms and ranches, and taking other protective measures.

Too Many Agencies? (pp. 363–364). Texas's Sunset Advisory Commission is an arm of the legislature. This 10-member commission (5 senators and 5 representatives) reviews each of the state's administrative agencies at 12-year intervals and makes recommendations to the legislature concerning continuation, abolition, or merger.

Looking Ahead (p. 364). Three trends in state administration seem likely to continue: accountability for efficient and economical performance in delivering public services, devolution of federal programs to state control and funding, and judicial actions to ensure that state policies comply with U.S. and Texas law.

C.   Key Terms (with textbook page numbers)

State Board of Education (SBOE) (337)

Texas Education Agency (TEA) (341)

Texas Assessment of Knowledge and Skills (TAKS) (342)

Texas Higher Education Coordinating Board (344)

executive commissioner of the Health and Human Services Commission (349)

Texas Department of Human Services (TDHS) (349)

Temporary Assistance for Needy Families (TANF) (349)

D.   Overview of the Readings (pp. 369–378)

8.1. "Capital Has Been Spent, But Education Post Shouldn't Be for Sale" (pp. 369–370)

This *Austin American-Statesman* editorial argues that the Texas Senate should reject Governor Rick Perry's nomination of Geraldine "Tincy" Miller to chair the
State Board of Education. It asserts that Miller is unqualified for four reasons: (1)
her opposition to efforts to deal with ethical violations by some board members and
with management problems related to the Permanent School Fund, (2) her attempts
to inappropriately influence textbook content, (3) the divisive politics she has prac-
ticed as a board member (especially the financial intervention of Miller and her
husband Vance that was designed to defeat SBOE chair Grace Shore in the 2002
Republican primary), and (4) her poor judgment in voting with the board's social
conservatives. The *American-Statesman* comments that Vance Miller's $50,000
contribution to Perry's 2002 gubernatorial campaign "did not go unnoticed" when
his wife was appointed to chair the SBOE.

8.2. "Schools of Hard Knocks" by Matt Flores (pp. 371–375)

State spending on public colleges and universities across Texas has often been un-
evenly distributed. Traditionally, South Texas has received less than other areas. To
remedy this injustice, in the 1990s the Texas Legislature funded the South Texas
Border Initiative. This involved an infusion of $500 million into institutions of
higher education located in South Texas. It was designed to increase educational
opportunities for residents (mostly Mexican Americans) within 41 counties along
or near the Rio Grande. The result was increased enrollments, new buildings, and
the addition of undergraduate majors and graduate programs. In 2003, however, the
10-year funding initiative was over, and the state faced a daunting budget shortfall
at the time this article was written. Although Texas has launched a "Closing the
Gaps" initiative for increasing minority enrollments by 2015, the special needs of

South Texas institutions of higher education must be met if gaps are to be closed for young people residing in South Texas and westward to El Paso.

8.3   "Is Plan Cutting Electric Costs?" by Sudeep Reddy (pp. 375–378)

After more than a year of deregulation, are Texas consumers of electricity better off? Under deregulation, public utilities like TXU in North Texas have had to pay attention to competition from other electric power providers. Nevertheless, prices for electricity remain high and appear to be heading to record levels. TXU blames this on higher natural gas prices, because much of the state's electricity is generated in gas-fueled power plants. Thus, TXU must ask the Public Utility Commission (PUC) to authorize rate increases that reflect higher gas prices. For competing providers, the PUC-approved rate becomes the "price to beat" as they seek to lure TXU's customers. While consumer groups point to record high rates, TXU notes that only a very small number of consumers have switched to other providers.

II.   *Testing Your Knowledge*

B.   True-False Questions on Text Material (with textbook page numbers)

_____   8.1.   The total of state FTE employees is less than the total of all personnel drawing paychecks from Texas state government. (334-335)

_____   8.2.   Texas has a centralized personnel system with uniform regulations and policies for all state employees. (335)

_____   8.3.   State employees work without paid vacations, holidays, or sick leave. (336)

_____   8.4.   Members of the State Board of Education are elected to represent 15 single-member districts. (337)

_____   8.5.   Charter schools in Texas are exempt from some state regulations. (341)

_____   8.6.   TAKS has been replaced by TASS for assessing students' mastery of state-mandated core curricula. (342)

_____   8.7.   The U.S. Supreme Court refused to review the *Hopwood* case concerning affirmative action for admission to the Law School of the University of Texas. (347–348)

_____   8.8.   The Texas Legislature has refused to appropriate money to combat the AIDS epidemic. (350)

_____   8.9.   Texas's 35 mental health community centers are entirely financed by county governments. (351)

_____ 8.10. A payroll tax provides revenue used for weekly benefit payments to unemployed workers who are covered by the Texas Unemployment Compensation Act. (351)

_____ 8.11. Most of the functions of the Texas Railroad Commission have nothing to do with railroads. (352)

_____ 8.12. The Office of Public Utility Counsel represents utility companies in rate cases heard by the Public Utility Commission. (353)

_____ 8.13. Under Texas law, one member of the commission heading the Texas Department of Transportation must have business ties with the transportation industry, one member must be a labor union member, and the third commissioner must be a "public member" without ties to the transportation industry or any labor union. (356)

_____ 8.14. The Texas Parks and Wildlife Commission sets fees for hunting licenses and fishing licenses. (357)

_____ 8.15. Texas industries produce less toxic contaminants than those of most other states. (358)

_____ 8.16. Creation of the Texas Natural Resource Conservation Commission (now Texas Commission on Environmental Quality) was one of the first projects of Governor George W. Bush. (358)

_____ 8.17. Texas's air pollution problems are confined to those caused by motor vehicles. (359)

_____ 8.18. Sites for the storage of high-level radioactive waste must be selected by the U.S. Department of Energy. (361)

_____ 8.19. Large federal grants for homeland security reached Texas soon after terrorist attacks on the World Trade Center and the Pentagon in September 2001. (362)

_____ 8.20. Texas's sunset process involves the systematic study of a state agency and then abolishing, merging, or retaining it. (363)

B. True-False Questions on Readings (with textbook page numbers)

_____ 8.21. Concerning Governor Perry's appointment of Geraldine "Tincy" Miller to chair the State Board of Education, the *Austin American Statesman* urged quick confirmation by the Senate. (369)

_____ 8.22. In 2002, helped by a big campaign contribution from Vance and "Tincy" Miller, Grace Shore was reelected to the State Board of Education. (369–370)

_____ 8.23. If the South Texas border region were to become a state, it would be the poorest in the nation. (372)

_____ 8.24. For many years South Texas lagged behind in development of institutions of higher education, but by the 1990s its universities offered several Ph.D. programs. (372)

_____ 8.25. Regulations of Texas's Public Utility Commission allow a fuel price adjustment if average natural gas prices go up 4 percent over a 10-day period. (376)

_____ 8.26. Half of the electricity marketed by Texas utilities is generated from nuclear and coal-fueled power plants. (377)

C. Multiple-Choice Questions on Text Material (with textbook page numbers)

_____ 8.27. People who need aid in obtaining service from the Texas bureaucracy may call the Citizen's Assistance (337)

    a. Hotline.
    b. Bank.
    c. Service.
    d. Depository.

_____ 8.28. Following the elections of 2000 and 2002, a majority of the members of the State Board of Education were (338)

    a. Anglo Democrats.
    b. Anglo Republicans.
    c. Latino Democrats.
    d. African-American Republicans.

_____ 8.29. Early in 2003, the newly appointed chair of the State Board of Education was (338-339)

    a. Linda Bauer.
    b. Vance Miller.
    c. Geraldine "Tincy" Miller.
    d. Grace Shore.

_____ 8.30. Members of the Texas Higher Education Coordinating Board are appointed to six-year terms by the (344)

    a. commissioner of education.
    b. governor.
    c. State Board of Education.
    d. chancellor of the University of Texas System.

8.31. In 2002, the Texas state university system with the most universities was (346)

a. the University of Houston System.
b. the Texas State University System.
c. the Texas A&M University System.
d. the University of Texas System.

8.32. A state law school can use race as a factor in admitting law students, according to the U.S. Supreme Court's 2003 ruling in (347–348)

a. *University of California Regents* v. *Bakke.*
b. *Hopwood* v. *Texas.*
c. *Grutter* v. *Bollinger.*
d. *Gratz* v. *Bollinger.*

8.33. The process whereby states (rather than the federal government) assume primary responsibility for administering programs such as welfare is called (348)

a. evolution.
b. revolution.
c. devolution.
d. convolution.

8.34. The federally funded and administered program that provides medical assistance for qualified applicants 65 years of age and older is called (349)

a. Medivac.
b. Mediflush.
c. Medicare.
d. Medicaid.

8.35. In January 2003, Texas health authorities reported more than 60,000 cumulative (350)

a. AIDS cases.
b. syphilis cases.
c. gonorrhea cases.
d. cancer cases.

_____ 8.36. Because mentally ill Texans must often wait years before receiving treatment in a Texas state mental health facility, many of them are (350)

    a.   lodged in hotels and motels at state expense.

    b.   detained in jails.

    c.   sent to state hospitals in other states.

    d.   sent to state hospitals in Mexico.

_____ 8.37. Each member of the Texas Workforce Commission (351)

    a.   receives a state salary.

    b.   represents employers.

    c.   is popularly elected for a term of six years.

    d.   is appointed by the lieutenant governor for a term of twelve years.

_____ 8.38. The Texas Railroad Commission functions in several capacities, but the primary area in which it is involved is (352)

    a.   farm and ranch issues.

    b.   oil and natural gas production.

    c.   railroad regulation.

    d.   coal production.

_____ 8.39. Belief that business practices should be governed by market conditions rather than by governmental rules leads logically to a policy of (353)

    a.   devolution.

    b.   deannexation.

    c.   deregulation.

    d.   dependence.

_____ 8.40. The date 1 December 2004 was set to mark the beginning of a largely deregulated system for automobile and homeowner insurance called (355)

    a.   "hide-and-seek."

    b.   "hit-and-run."

    c.   "swindle-and-cheat."

    d.   "file-and-use."

_____ 8.41. Texas's extensive state highway system is administered by the Texas (356)

    a.   Highway Department.

    b.   Good Roads Department.

    c.   Department of Transportation.

    d.   Department of Communication.

_____ 8.42. Fees for admission to Texas's state parks are set by (357)

    a. the legislature.

    b. the comptroller of public accounts.

    c. the state auditor.

    d. the Texas Parks and Wildlife Commission.

_____ 8.43. Control of water contamination is a major responsibility of (359)

    a. the Texas Water Development Board.

    b. the Texas Commission on Environmental Quality.

    c. the State Water Conservation Board.

    d. the Texas Water Well Drillers Board.

_____ 8.44. The Division of Emergency Management in the Governor's Office provides emergency response resources and information concerning (362)

    a. disaster preparedness.

    b. criminal activities involving terrorists.

    c. U.S. military operations in Iraq.

    d. U.S. diplomatic relations with governments suspected of promoting terrorism.

_____ 8.45. Final authority over whether to accept or reject a recommendation of the Sunset Advisory Commission lies with (363)

    a. the governor.

    b. the legislature.

    c. the head of the administrative agency that is affected.

    d. voters participating in a statewide referendum.

D.   Multiple-Choice Questions on Readings (with textbook page numbers)

_____ 8.46. The *Austin American-Statesman* charged that Geraldine "Tincy" Miller inappropriately influenced textbook content by advising publishers to consult with a conservative think tank in San Antonio, whose board members included (370)

    a. Hillary Clinton.

    b. Willie Nelson.

    c. Vance Miller.

    d. Laura Bush.

_____ 8.47. The *Austin American-Statesman* suggests that Geraldine "Tincy" Miller's appointment to chair the State Board of Education was influenced by her husband's $50,000 contribution to the election campaign of (370)

a. Tom Craddick.
b. David Dewhurst.
c. Tony Sanchez.
d. Rick Perry.

_____ 8.48. The Brownsville native who became President of the University of Texas—Brownsville is (371–373)

a. Ricardo Romo.
b. Rumaldo Juarez.
c. Juliet Garcia.
d. Ray Keck.

_____ 8.49. Of roughly 80,000 degrees conferred in Texas in 2002, the percent going to Hispanics was (375)

a. 32.0.
b. 16.4.
c. 11.0.
d. 7.0.

_____ 8.50. A year after partial deregulation of electric power rates, less than 7 percent of residential electricity consumers had (376)

a. changed electricity providers.
b. increased consumption of electric power.
c. indicated satisfaction with the rates that they were paying.
d. switched to use of natural gas.

_____ 8.51. The intent of deregulation of electric power rates is to go forward with (377)

a. government-owned power plants.
b. organization of electric power cooperatives.
c. market-based pricing.
d. nuclear power projects.

E. Completion Questions on Text Material (with textbook page numbers)

8.52. California has more state FTE _____ than Texas. (335)

8.53. San Jacinto Day is a state "skeleton crew" _____. (336)

8.54. The State Board of Education (SBOE) may reject a textbook or place it on one of two _____ lists for use in public schools. (339–340)

8.55. If a local school district fails to meet state standards, Texas Education Agency officials are permitted by law to assume _____ of that district temporarily until acceptable reforms are instituted. (341)

8.56. Duties of the Texas Higher Education Coordinating Board include responding to _____ for offering new academic programs and degrees. (346)

8.57. The Texas State University System does *not* have a _____ campus. (346)

8.58. Cheryl Hopwood sued the University of Texas after having been refused admission to its _____ school. (347)

8.59. Medicaid is designed to provide medical care for persons whose income places them below the _____ line. (349)

8.60. The Woman's, Infants, and Children (WIC) Program provides a delivery system for _____ packages. (350)

8.61. As the principal killer of Texas men in their thirties, no other public health problem rivals that of acquired immunodeficiency _____ (AIDS). (350)

8.62. Texas's welfare reform program emphasizes _____ responsibility for employment training. (351)

8.63. Green Mountain Energy Company and First Choice Power are retail _____ providers. (353)

8.64. Responsibility for preservation of Texas's natural habitat and providing recreational areas lies with the Texas _____ and Wildlife Commission. (357)

8.65. The Texas Water _____ Board is responsible for developing strategies for water conservation in the state. (360)

8.66. The Texas river with the largest volume of annual discharge into the Gulf of Mexico is the _____ River. (360)

8.67. A counterterrorism unit within the Texas Department of Public _____ handles reports of suspicious activities in which terrorists may be involved. (362)

8.68. In Texas, the Sunset Advisory Commission reviews each state agency every _____ years. (363)

F. Completion Questions on Readings (with textbook page numbers)

8.69. Money from Vance and Geraldine "Tincy" Millers' Prestonwood
_____ Club PAC was used to defeat Grace Shore in the 2002 Republican primary. (370)

8.70. Concerning Geraldine "Tinsy" Miller's service on the State Board of Education in recent years, the *Austin Amercan-Statesman* editorial complains that she "has become a reliable vote for the block of six social _____ ideologues." (370)

8.71. The South Texas university for which a school of pharmacy has been approved is Texas A&M—_____. (372)

8.72. Steve Murdock, Texas's demographer, says that the state's rapidly growing Hispanic population is on track to be _____educated in the future than it is today. (372)

8.73. Under Texas's electric restructuring plan, TXU's "price to beat" is locked in until at least 2005 or until it loses _____ percent of its original customers. (376)

8.74. Under Texas's electric restructuring plan, _____ users of electric power are paying far less than before deregulation. (378)

G. Essay Questions (with textbook page numbers)

1. Comment on the adequacy of pay and benefits for state employees in Texas. (335–336)
2. Describe the organization and responsibilities of the State Board of Education, and explain why it has been a center of controversy in recent years. (337–341)
3. Describe the responsibilities of the Texas Education Agency, and comment on Texas's experience with charter schools and with testing systems to determine student progress. (341–342)
4. Describe the organization and sources of funding for Texas's public institutions of higher education, and comment on their current problems and challenges. (342–348)
5. Identify state agencies and programs designed to assist Texans who are in need of publicly funded health and mental health care, temporary financial assistance, and help in finding employment. (348–351)
6. Identify the state agencies responsible for regulating Texas's oil and gas producers, public utilities, and insurance companies. Describe the organization of these regulatory agencies; and comment on the need for government regula-

tion or, on the other hand, the desirability of deregulation in favor of free-market solutions to problems in these areas. (351–356)

7. Explain the importance of Texas's highway system, state parks, and wildlife preservation efforts. (356–357).

8. Explain the need for environmental protection in Texas, and describe the responsibilities of the Texas Commission on Environmental Quality and the Texas Water Development Board in dealing with the state's problems involving air and water quality as well as disposal of hazardous waste. (358–361)

9. Explain why homeland security has become a matter of importance in Texas, and describe how costs for countering the terrorist threat are being funded. (361–363)

10. What is your opinion of the administrative structure and functioning of state government in Texas? Explain why you are satisfied or dissatisfied with the state's responses to selected public problems.

11. Using data in the How Do We Compare box at the top of page 335 of this chapter, rank the eight states in descending order according to the number of full-time equivalent (FTE) employees in each state. How does Texas rank?

12. Using data in the How Do We Compare box at the bottom of page 335 of this chapter, rank the eight states in descending order according to the average monthly pay per FTE employee. How does Texas rank? Is there an apparent relationship between rankings of states in #11 and #12? If so, what is your explanation of this relationship?

III. Applying Your Knowledge

A.   Outside Readings and Cartoons

1. From the endnotes for this chapter or from the updated bibliography of selected sources accessible through the Houghton Mifflin Political Science home page (politicalscience.college.hmco.com) choose a magazine article or journal article and write a summary of it.

2. From the endnotes for this chapter or from the updated bibliography of selected sources accessible through the Houghton Mifflin Political Science home page (politicalscience.college.hmco.com), choose a book and write a summary of one of its chapters.

3. In a newspaper, find an editorial that relates to the Texas state bureaucracy and/or matters concerning one or more state agencies. Summarize that editorial, and explain why you agree or disagree with the writer's point of view.

4. Find a newspaper article concerning the Texas state bureaucracy and/or one or more state agencies. Summarize that article, and describe what you do and/or do not like about this piece of reporting.

5. Interpret one of this chapter's cartoons (or another cartoon relating to a subject covered by the chapter), and explain why you agree or disagree with the cartoonist's point of view.

6. Explore two or more of the web sites listed among sources for this chapter. Then select one site and write a brief note outlining how its information contributes to your understanding of public policy and administration in Texas state government.

B. Internet Research Project

Objectives

1. To enhance awareness of the role of state agencies in regulating businesses in the state of Texas.

2. To introduce students to the assistance provided by the Office of the Comptroller of Public Accounts in creating new businesses through its web site.

3. To increase student knowledge of the variety of government-related issues that affect Texas businesses.

4. To provide students with alternative methods to reach a web page.

URL. http://www.window.state.tx.us/tba

Description of the Site. The comptroller of public accounts is responsible for collecting taxes and reporting on the fiscal condition of the state. To assist with economic growth in the state, the comptroller has created the *Texas Business Advisor.* This site includes information on issues that anyone opening a new business would need to consider. It is linked to state and federal agencies and provides access to forms, regulations, and data that would be helpful to a business person.

The comptroller's web site, *Window on State Government,* includes information about the Texas Performance Review (which is used to reorganize state agencies and make them more efficient), state agency performance, fiscal and economic conditions of the state (discussed in greater detail in Chapter 10 of this *Study Guide*), and links to related sites.

The internet is a dynamic, ever-changing environment. If any of the links and instructions need to be adjusted, consult the textbook web site for updates of this exercise (http://college.hmco.com/polisci/brown/prac_tex_pol/12e/students/index.html).

Use of Information. Assume that you are preparing to start a business related to your career goal. If you are planning to obtain a professional degree in law, medicine, architecture, or accounting, you may intend to open your own office. Anyone starting a business will have many questions about the likelihood that the business will succeed as well as what statutes and government agencies will affect the business and how.

In Texas, the comptroller has made it easy to get this information. You will find a number of topics that you should consider. In completing this exercise, pay close attention to the key words used in each question. They should lead you to the correct hyperlink. From the information available to you at this site, answer the following questions about your new business:

1. What type of business do you intend to create?

    _____

2. The first thing one would do in starting a business is to "Prepare". Follow the "prepare" link. What three steps would one take to prepare to start a business?

    a. _____

    b. _____

    c. _____

3. Back up to the Texas Business Advisor page. The second suggestion for "Growing a business" is to "Expand your client base." Follow that link. What two markets are suggested for expanding to?

    _____

4. Click on the "Back" icon and return to "The Texas Business Advisor" page. Click on "Take free—or, at least, low cost—advice." Click on the link "help" in the sentence "The state also provides help to small businesses." This will take you to the Texas Department of Economic Development's "Office of Small Business Assistance" page.

5. We now want to find out what permits and licenses you will need to start your business. Click on "Guide to Starting a Business." Click on "Step 3: Business Licenses and Permits by Business Type." Locate the type of business you want to start. Click on the first letter of the name of your profession or type of business. Scroll through the list until you find your profession or business. If your business does not appear to require special licensing or permits, be sure you have tried several terms to describe the business. If your business does not appear, choose another one that interests you. What is it?

    _____

6. From what state agency or agencies will you have to get special licenses or permits to conduct your business?

_____

_____

Internet Research Tip. Sometimes a web page will not connect. If you have typed the URL, double check to be sure there are no typographical errors in it because only the exact URL will connect to a site. If the URL is correct, it is possible that the web page has too many users trying to access it, or that it is being worked on, or that the URL has changed. Three strategies you might try are:

1. Entering the web page from a different path by erasing the URL to the previous slash and striking the "Enter" key. This page may give you a menu so that you can access the page you want.
2. Opening a search engine and conducting a query-driven search by typing the name of the organization or the web site into the query box. This method may give you a new URL for the page.
3. Simply come back at a different time. Sometimes web pages are unavailable because the page itself, or the server they are stored on, are being updated or worked on in some way (and thus are off-line).

Answers

True-False: Text		Multiple-Choice: Text		Completion: Text	
8.1.	T	8.27.	a	8.52.	employees
8.2.	F	8.28.	b	8.53.	holiday
8.3.	F	8.29.	c	8.54.	adoption
8.4.	T	8.30.	b	8.55.	control
8.5.	T	8.31.	d	8.56.	requests
8.6.	F	8.32.	c	8.57.	central
8.7.	T	8.33.	c	8.58.	law
8.8.	F	8.34.	c	8.59.	poverty
8.9.	F	8.35.	a	8.60.	food
8.10.	T	8.36.	b	8.61.	syndrome
8.11.	T	8.37.	a	8.62.	local
8.12.	F	8.38.	b	8.63.	electric
8.13.	F	8.39.	c	8.64.	Parks
8.14.	T	8.40.	d	8.65.	Development
8.15.	F	8.41.	c	8.66.	Sabine
8.16.	F	8.42.	d	8.67.	Safety
8.17.	F	8.43.	b	8.68.	12
8.18.	T	8.44.	a		
8.19.	F	8.45.	b		
8.20.	T				

True-False: Readings

Multiple-Choice: Readings

Completion: Readings

True-False: Readings		Multiple-Choice: Readings		Completion: Readings	
8.21.	F	8.46.	c	8.69.	Country
8.22.	F	8.47.	d	8.70.	conservative
8.23.	T	8.48.	c	8.71.	Kingsville
8.24.	F	8.49.	b	8.72.	less
8.25.	T	8.50.	a	8.73.	40
8.26.	T	8.51.	c	8.74.	big

CHAPTER NINE

Laws, Courts, and Justice

I.   *Preparing to Study*

A.   Performance Objectives

After studying and reviewing the text and readings in this chapter, you will be able to:

1. Identify categories of criminal offenses under Texas law.
2. Indicate the maximum fine and period of confinement possible for each category of criminal offense under Texas law.
3. Name the court or courts with original jurisdiction over each category of offense under Texas law.
4. Describe the organization and jurisdiction of each type of court in the Texas judicial system.
5. Describe the organization and functions of grand juries and trial juries under Texas law.
6. Outline the basic procedures followed in trying civil and criminal cases in Texas courts.
7. Outline the conditions under which a capital felony is committed.
8. Outline the questions that a jury must answer in determining the punishment for a capital offense.
9. Describe Texas's adult penal institutions and rehabilitation programs.
10. Describe Texas's juvenile justice system, giving special attention to procedures and institutions.
11. Identify selected problems and reforms (or proposed reforms) relating to crowded dockets, judicial selection, and rights of crime victims.

B.   Overview of the Text (pp. 380–430)

Early in the twenty-first century, Texas's legal system is affected by new developments in science and technology that influence the way justice is administered and the legal questions on which judges must rule.

An Introduction to Texas's Justice System (p. 380). Except for municipal court judges, members of the state's judiciary are popularly elected. Consequently, there is a close connection between politics and justice; but judges attract less public attention than legislators and executive officials.

State Law in Texas (pp. 380–382). There are more than 3,000 judges and almost that many courts in the Texas judicial system. Some hear civil law cases involving property, family issues, and personal injury; others hear criminal law cases; and many have jurisdiction over cases involving both civil disputes and criminal offenses. Courts with original jurisdiction try cases for the first time, but courts with appellate jurisdiction hear appeals after cases have been tried in lower courts. Some courts exercise both original and appellate jurisdiction.

Texas law includes state statutes, the Texas Constitution, and the common law dating back to medieval England. Statutory law is found in *Vernon's Revised Annotated Texas Civil Statute of the State of Texas,* in *General and Special Laws of the State of Texas* published after each legislative session, and in codes on broad topics found in *Vernon's Texas Codes.*

Courts, Judges, and Lawyers (pp. 382–398). The state's minor trial courts (municipal and justice-of-the-peace courts) are one-judge tribunals, as are county- and district-level courts. The number of judicial personnel on appellate courts varies. Each of the 14 courts of appeals has a chief justice and from two to twelve justices. The Court of Criminal Appeals has a presiding judge and eight judges, and the Supreme Court has a chief justice and eight justices. Municipal court judges are selected by methods and for terms specified by city charters. Other judges are popularly elected for terms of four years (justices of the peace and judges of county and district courts) or six years (judges and justices of appellate courts).

Traditional methods of disciplining delinquent judges involve trial by jury for judges at all levels and (for judges of district and higher courts) legislative address or impeachment by the House and removal by the Senate. In recent years, the State Commission on Judicial Conduct has handled most disciplinary matters.

About 70,000 lawyers are licensed to practice law in Texas. All of them must join and pay dues to the State Bar of Texas. Efforts to improve the image of lawyers among their fellow Texans include increased regulation by the State Bar and providing low-cost and pro bono legal services to poor people.

Juries (pp. 398–401). A citizen can participate in the administration of justice by serving on a grand jury or a trial jury. The former is composed of twelve people. They may be selected at random from a list of fifteen to twenty names. In most Texas counties, a three-member grand jury commission that is appointed by the district court judge prepares this list. Trial jurors are selected by attorneys from a venire panel that has been summoned. Twelve jurors are selected for a district court trial; six are selected for a trial before a lower court. The function of a grand jury is to return an indictment if the evidence indicates that an individual has committed a felony. A trial jury is responsible for listening to testimony and examining evidence to establish the guilt or innocence of a person charged with a crime or a party's liability in a civil case.

Judicial Procedures (pp. 402–412). In a civil proceeding, the plaintiff files a complaint with a court clerk. A citation is then served on the defendant, who files an answer. If either party so desires, a jury is selected to hear the case. After a verdict is reached, a judgment is issued. Appeal to a higher court is made on the basis of the trial court record and briefs submitted by interested parties. The Supreme Court of Texas is the highest state court having civil jurisdiction.

When the death penalty is assessed by a district court, the convicted person has an automatic right to appeal directly to the Court of Criminal Appeals. Fewer than 15 percent of these convictions are overturned on appeal. Since 1982, lethal injection has been used for all executions in Texas.

In a criminal trial, the prosecuting attorney calls witnesses and introduces evidence intended to support the charges. The defense may challenge the evidence, cross-examine witnesses, and present other evidence and witnesses on behalf of the defendant. A unanimous decision is required for a jury to reach a verdict. All convicted defendants are allowed to appeal to a higher court. The Court of Criminal Appeals is the highest state court exercising appellate criminal jurisdiction.

Correction and Rehabilitation (pp. 412–424). Convicted felons are usually imprisoned in facilities operated by the Institutional Division of the Texas Department of Criminal Justice (TDCJ). Some are confined in commercially operated, privatized facilities. Persons confined for state jail felonies are housed in state felony jails, which are designed for holding nonviolent offenders and providing alcohol and substance abuse treatment. Those incarcerated for Class A and Class B misdemeanor convictions, along with convicted felons awaiting transfer to a TDCJ facility, are held in a jail supervised by a county sheriff or in a commercially managed ("privatized") facility. State institutions of correction are supposed to serve the dual purpose of isolating offenders for the protection of society and rehabilitating them so that they will become law-abiding citizens when they are released from confinement.

Persons convicted of less serious offenses for the first time are usually placed under community supervision—that is, they are allowed to remain free as long as they comply with conditions imposed by the judge. Parole is a community-based rehabilitation program involving release of an inmate before completion of the imprisonment sentence.

Juvenile Justice (pp. 424–427). Generally, delinquent children who are at least 10 years of age but less than 17 years of age are subject to the laws of the Texas Family Code. Each county has a juvenile probation board that designates one or more juvenile judges and a chief juvenile probation officer. The board makes policies for a juvenile probation department that serves one or more counties. The Texas Juvenile Probation Commission oversees these county departments.

Juvenile offenders who are detained must be segregated from adult criminals. Counseling and probation are the principal means of dealing with juvenile offenders. Young offenders may be tried in juvenile courts. If a court finds that a youth has engaged in delinquent conduct and is in need of supervision, a disposition hearing is held. Youths who have committed serious offenses (or who have violated terms of probation) are confined in one of the Texas Youth Commission's training schools or in a boot camp. If paroled from a TYC facility, the parolee is required to continue in a program of supervised rehabilitation.

For felonies subject to the Juvenile Determinate Sentencing Law, a juvenile offender may serve part of a sentence in a TYC facility and then be transferred to TDCJ. Depending on age, juveniles may be tried as adults for commission of a capital offense or other felony and confined in a TDCJ prison.

Problems and Reforms: Implications for Public Policy (pp. 427–430). Many reforms have been made in the Texas system of law and justice; others have been proposed but not adopted or implemented. Because justice delayed is justice denied, the legislature has continued to expand the number of courts and judges. Other attempts to cope with crowded dockets include transferring cases from overburdened courts to courts with fewer pending cases, assigning active and retired judges to courts with crowded dockets, and using various alternative dispute resolution (ADR) processes to settle disputes in a more informal environment.

People who are dissatisfied with partisan election of judges have advocated nonpartisan elections or a Missouri Plan system. The Missouri Plan features a combination of appointment and election of judges. The Texas Legislature has repeatedly rejected such proposals.

The Texas Constitution has been amended to guarantee the rights of crime victims. A crime victims compensation program helps people who have lost wages and incurred expenses as a result of injuries inflicted on them by adult criminals or juvenile delinquents.

Looking Ahead (p. 430). Although the Texas legal system is complex, citizens should understand it. Ordinary Texans, as well as our lawyers and judges, are affected by the state's laws, courts, and penal institutions.

C. **Key Terms** (with textbook page numbers)

civil law (381)	petition (403)
criminal law (381)	defendant (403)
jurisdiction (381)	special issues (404)
original jurisdiction (381)	verdict (404)
appellate jurisdiction (381)	judgment (404)
exclusive jurisdiction (382)	graded penalties (405)
concurrent jurisdiction (382)	capital felony (405)
court of record (385)	felony (405)
small claims court (387)	misdemeanor (405)
probate (388)	recidivism (417)
grand jury (398)	charitable choice (424)
petit jury (399)	alternative dispute resolution (ADR)
venire (400)	(427)
voir dire (400)	Missouri Plan (428)
tort (400)	appointment-retention system (429)
plaintiff (403)	

D. **Overview of the Readings** (pp. 434–438)

9.1. "In Drug Court, Success Is Sweet" by Thom Marshall (pp. 434–435)

An innovative program of the Fort Bend County Drug Court rewards its charges with Life Savers candy. Each participant who has completed court-ordered requirements since the last meeting—including testing drug free—gets a Life Saver. Anyone who has failed to comply with rules of the program, such as arriving late for a court-ordered drug treatment meeting, is given the choice of a candy and community service, or no candy and no service. Unless all participants earn a Life Saver, either through meeting requirements or by compensating with community service, each member of the group is fined a dollar. The amount of the fine is small, but the candy is a symbol of success and the key to earning peer respect. This court, one of seven drug courts in Texas (as of early 2003) and more than 900 throughout the country, offers judicial oversight together with drug treatment. Participants learn to make decisions and to take responsibility. And, if they complete the program successfully, their criminal record is expunged.

9.2. "A Caring Mom's Idea Led to Plan" by Bud Kennedy (pp. 435–438)

When a child is abducted, information concerning anyone seen near the child can be critical for a search effort. One mother, hearing about the loss of another mother's child, was led to suggest what will become a nationwide cooperative effort of radio stations helping to find missing children. It is named the Amber Alert in memory of Amber Hagerman, whose abduction and murder sparked Diane Simone's idea. As soon as a child is missing, law enforcement officials can begin emergency broadcasts asking for information and giving descriptions of suspicious people and vehicles. By alerting the public, the police mobilize many sets of eyes to look for the missing child. While Simone is reluctant to take credit for the idea, she is overjoyed at the number of children who have been found and returned to their homes.

II. *Testing Your Knowledge*

A. **True-False Questions on Text Material** (with textbook page numbers)

_____ 9.1. Under the Texas Constitution, a court has either original jurisdiction or appellate jurisdiction but never both. (381)

_____ 9.2. All justices of the peace who fail to complete mandatory instruction on the performance of their duties are removed from office. (386)

_____ 9.3. None of Texas's justices of the peace devotes full time to this judicial office. (386)

_____ 9.4. Under Texas law, a JP court's judgment for $20 or less cannot be appealed to a higher court of the state. (388)

_____ 9.5. A party to a suit in a small claims court in Texas must be represented by a lawyer. (387)

_____ 9.6. Only a few of Texas's district court judges initially get their jobs by gubernatorial appointment. (389)

_____ 9.7. State district courts have jurisdiction over misdemeanor cases involving misconduct by government officials while acting in an official capacity. (389)

_____ 9.8. A significant part of the work of the Supreme Court of Texas concerns handling applications for a writ of error. (393)

_____ 9.9. Under Texas law, impeachment by the House and removal by the Senate are the only legal ways to discipline a state judge or justice. (394)

_____ 9.10. The Supreme Court of Texas appoints members of the Board of Law Examiners. (395)

_____ 9.11. Grand jurors in all Texas counties are selected by a judge from a list prepared by a jury commission. (398)

_____ 9.12. Daily pay for all jurors is fixed at $10 by Texas law. (401)

_____ 9.13. Torts include injuries and damages caused by the acts of individuals and corporations. (402)

_____ 9.14. For a verdict to be reached in a Texas civil proceeding, all members of the jury must be in agreement. (404)

_____ 9.15. Under Texas law, a third felony conviction may result in a sentence of imprisonment for life. (405)

_____ 9.16. Since 1982, capital punishment under Texas law has meant death in the state's electric chair. (409)

_____ 9.17. Except in a capital felony case where the prosecutor is seeking the death penalty, a criminal defendant may waive the right to a jury trial if the prosecuting attorney agrees. (411)

_____ 9.18. In a jury trial of a criminal case conducted under Texas law, the sentence may be fixed by the jury if the convicted person so requests. (411)

_____ 9.19. The Texas Department of Criminal Justice is headed by three elected, state-salaried commissioners. (414)

_____ 9.20. Every Texas county maintains a jail. (420)

_____ 9.21. In Texas, adult first-time offenders convicted of misdemeanors and lesser felonies are commonly placed under community supervision. (421)

_____ 9.22. Supervising the rehabilitation and training of delinquent children is the responsibility of the Texas Youth Commission (TYC). (425)

_____ 9.23. On the request of a Texas crime victim, that victim has the right to receive recent information about proceedings affecting the criminal and to provide input into parole decisions regarding that offender. (430)

B. True-False Questions on Readings (with textbook page numbers)

_____ 9.24. Studies show that every public dollar spent on drug courts saves nearly $10. (434)

_____ 9.25. Fort Bend County's drug court program is designed to teach offenders to weigh options and make good personal decisions. (435)

_____ 9.26. One inspiration for the Amber Plan was the quick return of a lost child in New York City. (436)

_____ 9.27. Abduction cases frequently involve children who are put into vehicles and transported from the point of abduction to another point. (437)

C. **Multiple-Choice Questions on Text Material** (with textbook page numbers)

_____ 9.28. A Texas court's authority to hear a case for the first time is defined as (381)

    a. civil jurisdiction.
    b. criminal jurisdiction.
    c. original jurisdiction.
    d. appellate jurisdiction.

_____ 9.29. Located at the base of the Texas judicial structure are justice-of-the-peace courts and (483)

    a. municipal courts.
    b. constitutional county courts.
    c. district courts.
    d. county courts at law.

_____ 9.30. A trial de novo involves (385-386)

    a. a jury composed of nine people.
    b. a new trial.
    c. a trial conducted under Spanish law.
    d. judicial review of the law but not the facts involved in a case.

_____ 9.31. Serving subpoenas and other processes issued by trial courts in Texas is the principal function of most (386)

    a. coroners.
    b. deputy sheriffs.
    c. constables.
    d. rangers.

_____ 9.32. The criminal jurisdiction of a justice-of-the-peace court covers (386)

    a. class A misdemeanors.
    b. class B misdemeanors.
    c. class C misdemeanors.
    d. felonies.

_____ 9.33. Texas's county courts at law are also called (388)

    a. constitutional county courts.
    b. statutory courts.
    c. misdemeanor courts.
    d. appellate county courts.

9.34. In the event of death, resignation, or removal of a state district judge, the vacancy is filled by (389)

    a. a special election called by the governor.

    b. an appointment made by the chief justice of the Supreme Court of Texas.

    c. an appointment made by the governor.

    d. an appointment made by the attorney general.

9.35. Appeal following a capital felony conviction in a state district court is taken to (391)

    a. a court of appeals.

    b. the Supreme Court of Texas.

    c. the Court of Criminal Appeals.

    d. a statutory court.

9.36. The presiding judge of the Texas Court of Criminal Appeals is (392)

    a. appointed by the lieutenant governor.

    b. selected by the other members of that court.

    c. appointed by the attorney general.

    d. popularly elected to that office unless appointed by the governor to fill a vacancy.

9.37. The Texas Constitution guarantees that everyone charged with a crime is entitled to (396)

    a. absence from work with full pay by the employer until the case is resolved.

    b. compensation by the state for lost salary or wages until the case is resolved.

    c. representation by an attorney.

    d. free transportation from the defendant's home to the court where the case is tried.

9.38. Under Texas law, which of the following is a qualification for jurors? (399)

    a. Minimum age of 18 years

    b. Graduate of a high school

    c. No prior indictment or accusation of theft

    d. Maximum age of 70 years

_____ 9.39. Unless disapproved by the legislature, rules of civil procedure for Texas courts are made by the state's (403)

    a. attorney general.
    b. Supreme Court.
    c. bar association.
    d. justices of courts of civil appeals.

_____ 9.40. The Texas system of graded penalties for criminal offenses features punishments for classes A, B, and C (405)

    a. state jail felonies.
    b. capital felonies.
    c. felonies.
    d. misdemeanors.

_____ 9.41. After a Texas jury has found a defendant guilty of a capital offense, it must then decide whether (408)

    a. the victim and the offender were of the same religion or political party.
    b. a firearm was used by the defendant.
    c. the victim and the offender were of the same race or ethnic group.
    d. there is a possibility that the defendant will commit criminal acts of violence that would constitute a continuing threat to society.

_____ 9.42. When the accused pleads guilty in return for the promise that the prosecution will seek a lighter sentence or will recommend probation, it is said that the attorneys in the case have engaged in (411)

    a. corruption.
    b. plea bargaining.
    c. nolo contendere.
    d. probation.

_____ 9.43. In a criminal case, a judge may refuse to accept the verdict of the trial jury and (411)

    a. pardon the accused.
    b. substitute the judge's own verdict for that of the jury.
    c. refer the case to a higher court for a verdict.
    d. order a new trial.

9.44. In *Ruiz* v. *Estelle* (1980), U.S. District Court Judge William Wayne Justice (418)

    a. condemned overcrowding in Texas prison units.
    b. closed the substandard facilities of the Texas Youth Commission.
    c. ruled that Texas judges and justices must be elected in single-member districts.
    d. ruled that all people charged with crimes must be released on bail pending trial.

9.45. Texas's system of state felony jails has been designed to house (419)

    a. persons convicted of capital felonies.
    b. persons convicted of aggravated offenses.
    c. nonviolent offenders.
    d. persons convicted of class C misdemeanors.

9.46. When a jail or prison sentence is commuted to community supervision, the convicted person (421)

    a. is assigned to a halfway house.
    b. receives a conditional pardon.
    c. is disinherited.
    d. is not confined if the terms of supervision are fulfilled.

9.47. Texas's Juvenile Determinate Sentencing Law allows sentences for as long as 40 years for juveniles who commit serious offenses like (426)

    a. flight to avoid arrest.
    b. capital murder.
    c. theft of property valued at $1,500 or more but less than $20,000.
    d. juvenile gang activities.

9.48. Mediation is one of the procedures utilized under Texas's system of (427)

    a. alternative dispute resolution.
    b. crime victim assistance.
    c. disciplining judges and justices.
    d. regulating attorneys.

9.49. Responsibility for administering Texas's Crime Victims Compensation Act rests with the state's (429)

    a. Department of Criminal Justice.
    b. Department of Public Safety.
    c. attorney general.
    d. Workers' Compensation Commission.

D. Multiple-Choice Questions on Readings (with textbook page numbers)

_____ 9.50. Offenders supervised by the Fort Bend County Drug Court may compensate for violation of court rules by (434)

   a. performing community service.
   b. laying out a fine at the rate of $10 per day.
   c. paying a fine of $1.
   d. making a public apology.

_____ 9.51. Drug court programs combine judicial oversight with (434)

   a. supervised treatment.
   b. corporal punishment.
   c. confinement in jail.
   d. chain-gang labor.

_____ 9.52. The Amber Plan is named for Amber Hagerman, (435)

   a. a policewoman in Arlington.
   b. a Texas girl who was abducted and murdered.
   c. a member of the Texas Legislature.
   d. a radio station manager in Fort Worth.

_____ 9.53. The Amber Plan proposal was set forth originally in a letter from Diana Simone to (437–438)

   a. a radio station manager.
   b. a police chief.
   c. a massage parlor operator.
   d. a Southern Baptist minister.

E. Completion Questions on Text Material (with textbook page numbers)

9.54. Prosecution of someone charged with theft would involve _____ law. (381)

9.55. Texas's justices of the peace and municipal court judges serve as _____ of the state when they issue warrants for the arrest of suspects. (382)

9.56. Municipal court judges are authorized to impose maximum fines of $_____ in cases involving violations of some city ordinances. (385)

9.57. Every Texas county is divided into one to _____ justice-of-the-peace precincts. (386)

9.58. According to the Texas Constitution, the judge of a constitutional county court is supposed to be "well informed in the _____ of the state." (387)

9.59. Establishing the validity of a will for a person who has died is a _____ matter. (388)

9.60. Texas's criminal district courts in Dallas, Tarrant, and Jefferson counties have general jurisdiction that extends to _____ as well as criminal cases. (390)

9.61. The legislature has divided Texas into 14 state court of _____ districts. (391)

9.62. The highest court in Texas with criminal jurisdiction is the Court of _____ Appeals. (391)

9.63. To maintain their active status in Texas, practicing attorneys must complete at least 15 hours of continuing education each year, including three hours of legal _____. (395)

9.64. One member of each Texas grand jury is appointed to serve as its _____. (398)

9.65. The party that initiates a civil suit by filing a petition is known as the _____. (403)

9.66. In order for a Texas jury to reach a verdict of guilty or not guilty in a criminal case, a _____ decision must be reached. (411)

9.67. Most of the inmates of facilities operated by the TDCJ's State _____ Division are intended to undergo treatment for drug and alcohol abuse. (414)

9.68. Highlighting developments concerning Texas's prison system in the decade before the Texas Department of Corrections became the Texas Department of Criminal Justice was U.S. District Court Judge William Wayne Justice's ruling in _____ v. *Estelle*. (418)

9.69. Violent inmates held in administrative _____ cells primarily live in isolation from other prisoners. (418-419)

9.70. The Texas Commission on _____ Standards establishes standards for privately operated jails. (421)

9.71. Under Texas law, offenders who are at least 10 years of age but less than 17 years of age are generally treated as "_____ children" if they commit prohibited acts. (424)

9.72. Texas law helps a crime _____ collect compensation for expenses incurred as a result of injuries suffered at the hands of criminals. (429)

F.   Completion Questions on Readings (with textbook page numbers)

9.73. Successful completion of the Fort Bend County Drug Court's program results in no _____ record. (434)

9.74. Offenders in the Fort Bend Drug Court's program are helped in their recovery efforts by a group of _____. (435)

9.75. Rev. Tom Stoker believes that Diana Simone ought to be recognized as the _____ of the Amber Plan. (436)

9.76. With the help of law enforcement agencies, creation of the Amber Plan involved work by the Dallas/Fort Worth Association of _____ Managers. (437)

G.   Essay Questions (with textbook page numbers)

1. Describe the organization and jurisdiction of each of the following lower-level courts in the Texas judicial pyramid—justice-of-the-peace courts, constitutional county courts, and county courts at law—and outline the terms of office, qualifications, and methods of selection for the judges in these courts. (382–388)
2. Describe the organization and jurisdiction of Texas's district-level courts and courts of appeals. In addition, describe the qualifications and methods of selection for judges of these courts. (388–391)
3. Compare Texas's Court of Criminal Appeals and the Supreme Court of Texas with regard to organization, personnel, and jurisdiction. (391–394)
4. Describe the role of the Commission on Judicial Conduct in disciplining Texas judges and justices. (394–395)
5. Write an essay entitled "Lawyers and the Legal Profession in Texas." Include in this essay problems involving legal services for the poor. (395–397)
6. Assume that you have been summoned as a prospective juror who may be selected for jury duty on a noncapital felony case to be tried in a Texas court. Describe the qualifications for jurors and explain the processes involved in selecting the jury, conducting the trial, determining guilt or innocence of the accused, and assessing punishment (if the defendant is convicted). (399–401 and 409–411)
7. Write an essay entitled "Capital Punishment Under Texas Law." In your essay, list six crimes punishable by death, and describe the process by which a jury determines whether a death sentence should be imposed. (405–409)

8. Describe Texas's system for correction and rehabilitation of adult criminals who are confined in prison units and state felony jails throughout the state. (412–420)

9. Describe Texas's community-based programs for dealing with convicted adult criminals, and comment on some policy issues involving community supervision and parole. (421–424)

10. Write an essay entitled "A Survey of the Juvenile Justice System in Texas." Include descriptions of agencies, procedures, and institutions designed to deal with juvenile delinquents. In conclusion, express your opinions concerning the effectiveness of the state's juvenile justice policies. (424–427)

11. Discuss the issue of judicial selection, explaining different views on the Texas system of popular election (except for some municipal court judges) and alternative means of selection, such as that provided by the Missouri Plan. (428–429)

12. Using data in the How Do We Compare box at the top of page 392 of this chapter, rank the states in descending order according to annual salaries for the associate justices/judges of their highest courts. How does Texas rank?

13. Using data in the How Do We Compare box at the top of page 407 of this chapter, rank the states in descending order according to number of executions from 1976 through February 2003. Where does Texas rank?

III. Applying Your Knowledge

A. Outside Readings and Cartoons

1. From the endnotes for this chapter or from the updated bibliography of selected sources accessible through the Houghton Mifflin Political Science home page (politicalscience.college.hmco.com) choose a magazine article or journal article and write a summary of it.

2. From the endnotes for this chapter or from the updated bibliography of selected sources accessible through the Houghton Mifflin Political Science home page (politicalscience.college.hmco.com), choose a book and write a summary of one of its chapters.

3. Find an editorial that relates to Texas laws, courts, or correction policies. Summarize that editorial, and explain why you agree or disagree with the writer's point of view.

4. Find a newspaper article concerning Texas laws, courts, or correction policies. Summarize the article, and describe what you do and/or do not like about this piece of reporting.

5. Interpret one of this chapter's cartoons (or another cartoon concerning laws, courts, and justice), and explain why you agree or disagree with the cartoonist's point of view.

6. Explore two or more of the Web sites listed among sources for this chapter. Then select one site and write a brief note outlining how its information contributes to your understanding of Texas law, courts, and justice.

B.   Internet Research Project

Objectives

1. To introduce students to the legal information available at the University of Houston Law Center's People's Lawyer site.

2. To make students familiar with the Texas judiciary's web sites, visit the sites of the Texas Supreme Court and Court of Criminal Appeals, and note the gender make-up of Texas's highest courts.

2. To familiarize students with electronic mail.

3. To enhance student ability to research information from different hyperlinked sites and pages.

URLs   http://www.law.uh.edu/peopleslawyer
         http://www.courts.state.tx.us

Description of the Sites. The first site, The People's Lawyer, is intended to make the law accessible to those without legal background or training. The University of Houston Law Center maintains the site. Its features include a lawyer referral list for low-cost and pro bono legal services, links to other law-related sites, and a series of pages on legal topics authored by Professor Richard M. Alderman. Hyperlinks are also provided to a number of primary legal documents that include court decisions, statutes, and administrative regulations. Sites of interest to a particular group, such as senior citizens, are also hyperlinked.

Information is available on "The People's Law School," a biannual program offered free to the general public at the University of Houston Law Center. The purpose of the project is to make the law "user friendly." Classes are offered on criminal law, family law, suing in small claims court, landlord/tenant law, and similar areas of the law that affect individuals on a daily basis. If you are unable to attend these classes, the site also has an option for you. Professor Alderman has written a number of articles on legal topics including suing in small claims court, living wills, and tenant rights. Further, he has answered questions about typical legal problems that people have. If you have a question that has not been previously answered, you can submit your inquiry to Professor Alderman by e-mail. His e-mail address is available on the site. Topics are added frequently, so many more legal issues may be addressed by the time you review the site.

The second site, Texas Judiciary Online, is a state judicial system web page. It is a project of the Judicial Committee on Information Technology and the Office of Court Administration. This site serves as a home page for the Texas courts and judicial agencies, providing links to federal courts and other legal resources.

The internet is a dynamic, ever-changing environment. If any of the links and instructions need to be adjusted, consult the textbook web site for updates of this exercise (http://college.hmco.com/polisci/brown/prac_tex_pol/12e/students/index.html).

Use of Information. Begin at the home page for The People's Lawyer web site (http://www.law.uh.edu/peopleslawyer). Answer the following questions based on information that you find by moving among the hyperlinked pages and sites.

1. Click on the hypertext "Common Q and A's." Open the drop-down menu and Go to the word Miscellaneous. Review the list of topics, paying special attention to the words used in each question. Can my bank charge for a bounced check?

   _____

2. Click on the "Back" icon and choose "Family/Divorce" from the drop down menu. Go there. How can a seventeen-year-old legally move out if the parents object?

   _____

3. Click on the "Back" icon, and choose "Real Estate/Landlord/Tenant." Go there. Who must pay for the batteries in a smoke detector—the landlord or the tenant?

   _____

4. Go to the bottom of the page and click on the hypertext "Back to the People's Lawyer Homepage." Click on the hypertext "Death and Dying Issues." Go to that portion of the page that discusses the Medical Power of Attorney. Click on "Medical Power of Attorney for Health Care." Many people who have living wills also have a medical power of attorney. What is the purpose of a medical power of attorney?

   _____

5. Click on the "Back" icon. Go to the bottom of the page and click on the hypertext "Back to the People's Lawyer Homepage." You should now be on the home page. Click on the hypertext "Small Claims Court," and then on "What Do I Do After I Win." If you win a suit in small claims court and the defen-

dant does not pay, what are two things you can do to try to collect your judgment?

(1) _____

(2) _____

6. We also want to look at the two highest state courts in Texas. Go to Texas Judiciary Online (http://www.courts.state.tx.us). Then click on "TJ Online Home." Click on "Supreme Court of Texas" link on the bottom of the page. Locate the button labeled "Justices" and click it.

    a. How many female Supreme Court justices are there?

        _____

    b. How many male Supreme Court justices are there?

        _____

7. Click on the "Back" icon twice. You should now be back on the Texas Judiciary on-line homepage. Click on "Court of Criminal Appeals" link on the bottom of the page. Click on the hypertext "Judges."

    a. How many female members of the Court of Criminal Appeals are there?

        _____

    b. How many male members of the Court of Criminal Appeals are there?

        _____

Internet Research Tip. Two ways to reach Richard Alderman with your legal questions are included in this site. One is by "snail mail," or postal mail. The other is by electronic mail, or e-mail. Electronic mail has been the leading use of the Internet, providing a quick and efficient way to contact anyone else in the world who also has e-mail. You need a computer, an e-mail address, and a connection to the Internet to use electronic mail. Your college or university may provide its students with e-mail accounts. Most Internet service providers (private companies that offer Internet access to individuals) include electronic mail as one of their benefits.

The e-mail form provided at this site includes the information Alderman requires for legal questions. You must include your street address and your e-mail address. When you click on the "Submit Question" bar, your request is automatically sent to him. His e-mail address is also included on the web page. The address can be divided into a user name **(peopleslawyer)**, the connector "at" **(@)**, a server name **(www.law.uh)**, and a domain name **(.edu)**. No spaces are used in an address. Some addresses include an underscore character **(_)**. Again, a space is not substituted for this character. If you are unable to remember an e-mail address, ask the individual to send you electronic mail. You can capture the other person's address from that message.

Answers

True-False: Text		Multiple-Choice: Text		Completion: Text	
9.1.	F	9.28.	c	9.54.	criminal
9.2.	F	9.29.	a	9.55.	magistrates
9.3.	F	9.30.	b	9.56.	2,000
9.4.	T	9.31.	c	9.57.	eight
9.5.	F	9.32.	c	9.58.	law
9.6.	F	9.33.	b	9.59.	probate
9.7.	T	9.34.	c	9.60.	civil
9.8.	T	9.35.	c	9.61.	appeals
9.9.	F	9.36.	d	9.62.	Criminal
9.10.	T	9.37.	c	9.63.	ethics
9.11.	F	9.38.	a	9.64.	foreman
9.12.	F	9.39.	b	9.65.	plaintiff
9.13.	T	9.40.	d	9.66.	unanimous
9.14.	F	9.41.	d	9.67.	Jail
9.15.	T	9.42.	b	9.68.	Ruiz
9.16.	F	9.43.	d	9.69.	segregation
9.17.	T	9.44.	a	9.70.	Jail
9.18.	T	9.45.	c	9.71.	delinquent
9.19.	F	9.46.	d	9.72.	victim
9.20.	F	9.47.	b		
9.21.	T	9.48.	a		
9.22.	T	9.49.	c	Completion: Readings	
9.23.	T			9.73.	criminal

True-False: Readings		Multiple-Choice: Readings			
				9.74.	peers
9.24.	T	9.50.	a	9.75.	mother
9.25.	T	9.51.	a	9.76.	Radio
9.26.	F	9.52.	b		
9.27.	T	9.53.	a		

CHAPTER TEN

Revenues, Expenditures, and Fiscal Policy

I. *Preparing to Study*

A. Performance Objectives

After studying and reviewing the text and readings in this chapter, you will be able to:

1. Identify important changes in the Texas economy from the 1980s to the early years of the twenty-first century.
2. Describe important demands and pressures that have influenced the formulation of state fiscal policies regarding public schools, highways, prisons, and welfare programs.
3. Outline traditional Texas policies on budgeting, taxing, and spending.
4. Outline the principal steps in preparing, adopting, and implementing a budget for the state of Texas.
5. Identify the principal agencies of Texas state government with special responsibilities for collecting taxes, investing public funds, making and supervising state purchases, overseeing the management of the state's money, and auditing state accounts.
6. Identify the principal sources of state tax revenues (excluding gambling revenues) under Texas law, and describe the relative importance of each.
7. Describe the forms of legalized gambling in Texas, and note the relative importance of each as a source of state revenue.
8. Identify the principal sources of state nontax revenues under Texas law, and describe the relative importance of each.
9. Discuss Texas's bonded indebtedness, giving special attention to the different types of state bonds.
10. Illustrate and describe the politics of public spending in Texas for public schools, colleges, and universities.
11. Illustrate and describe the politics of public spending for human services, public transportation, and public safety.

B. Overview of the Text (pp. 440–483)

Fiscal policy concerns taxing, spending, borrowing, and managing the state government's money.

Looking Back (pp. 440–442). Texas entered the twentieth century with an economy that was primarily based on cattle and cotton. Then oil became an economic mainstay for Texas business and provided large amounts of revenue for state government. After devastating drops in oil prices during the 1980s, the Texas economy became more diversified. Many workers took jobs in the service sector, and state government became increasingly dependent on sales tax revenue. Meanwhile, policymakers faced the following problems: continuing population growth; increasing numbers of poor families; rising costs of education, medical care, and prisons; mandates for more public spending; and continuing revenue shortfalls.

In the last years of the twentieth century, the Texas economy was healthier than that of the nation as a whole. By the opening of the twenty-first century, however, Texas was experiencing the same economic ills that plagued other parts of the country. Thus, legislators and other state officials were confronted with a wide range of critical problems that included the following: declining lottery profits, decreasing revenue from tobacco taxes, expanding tax-free e-commerce, rising demands for a better-educated workforce, swelling costs of medical treatment for the prison population, and increasing needs for social services for all aging Texans.

Enduring Policy Issues (pp. 442–446). Four major issues attracted the attention of Texans from the 1980s to 2003: equalizing funding between the richest and the poorest school districts, meeting funding requirements for highway maintenance and construction despite insufficient appropriations and increased highway deterioration, housing a large prison population, and deciding who among the poor would receive welfare assistance and how much.

Traditional Fiscal Policies (pp. 446–450). Trying to respond to fiscal crises, Texas's policymakers have struggled to operate the state's government on a balanced budget while seeking to keep a low level of taxation and to hold down public spending.

Politics of Budgeting and Fiscal Management (pp. 450–458). Planning and supervising state expenditures involve preparing and adopting the state budget, accounting for state funds, purchasing equipment and supplies for state agencies, and auditing records of receipts and expenditures. The comptroller of public accounts is the state's chief tax collector, but various taxes and fees are collected in other departments. Administration of the Texas lottery is the responsibility of the Texas Lottery Commission.

Politics of Revenue and Debt Management (pp. 458–472). Sales taxes account for the largest portion of state tax revenue in Texas. The state imposes not only a general sales tax but also selective sales taxes on such items as motor fuels, alcoholic beverages, cigarettes, and motor vehicles. Business taxes include taxes on corporate franchises, gross receipts, and extraction of certain minerals (such as severance taxes on production of oil and natural gas). Nevertheless, the tax burden of Texans is lighter than the national average.

Revenue is collected by the state from three types of gambling operations: horse and dog racing, a state-managed lottery, and bingo. Texas's nontax revenues include federal grants-in-aid, money borrowed by selling bonds, income from state-owned land, damages paid to the state by tobacco companies, and revenue from miscellaneous sources.

Through constitutional amendments, Texans have authorized the sale of self-liquidating revenue bonds and limited-obligation bonds to finance the purchase of homes as well as farms and ranches by veterans, to provide loans to college and university students, to build new prisons, and to construct university buildings. Projects financed with bond money must be approved by the Texas Legislature and by the five-member Texas Bond Review Board.

Politics of Spending (pp. 472–482). For many years, state expenditures for education have exceeded those for other budget items. Public education for more than 4 million school children (kindergarten through high school) is largely administered by more than a thousand locally elected school boards. Attempts to equalize opportunities for Texas children to obtain an adequate public school education have produced a succession of legislative acts and judicial rulings, but unresolved problems remain. Meanwhile, enrollments in institutions of public education at all levels (including community colleges and state universities) require the annual expenditure of many billions of dollars of state funds.

Although the federal government now makes all direct-assistance payments to the blind, the permanently and totally disabled, and people receiving old-age assistance, Texas is responsible for administering Temporary Assistance for Needy Families (TANF). Expenditures for health and human services constitute the state's second largest budget item, followed by highway construction and maintenance. Spending on prisons increased significantly during the 1990s.

Looking Ahead (pp. 482–483). Although "no new taxes" and budget slashing were fiscal policies of Governor Rick Perry and the GOP-controlled legislature in 2003, policies for the future are likely to feature new taxes, increases in some tax rates, more state responsibility for programs jointly funded with the federal government, and deferral of capital construction, maintenance, and renovation. Much will depend on the state's economic circumstance as affected by national and international developments beyond the control of Texas policymakers. Fiscal crises are inevitable and will test the ability of state officials to respond with appropriate taxing, spending, and borrowing.

C. Key Terms (with textbook page numbers)

fiscal policy (440)
service-sector jobs (441)
Robin Hood plan (442)
underemployment (445)
Children's Health Insurance Program
    (CHIP) (445)
balanced budget (447)
casual deficit (447)
General Revenue Fund (447)
regressive taxes (448)
progressive taxes (448)
fiscal management process (450)
budget (450)
Legislative Budget Board (LBB) (450)
current-services based budget (451)
fiscal notes (451)
dual budgeting system (454)
budget execution (454)
special fund (457)
cash accounting (457)
state auditor (458)
tax (458)
selective sales tax (459)
general sales tax (460)

sin tax (461)
general business tax (462)
selective business tax (462)
corporate franchise tax (462)
payroll tax (462)
severance tax (463)
crude oil production tax (463)
gas gathering tax (463)
gross receipts tax (463)
gross premium tax (463)
insurance administration tax (463)
death tax (463)
grant-in-aid (467)
securitization (469)
bonded debt (471)
"rainy day" fund (472)
Texas Mobility Fund (472)
functional expenditure (473)
objective expenditure (473)
Texas Tomorrow Fund (477)
TEXAS Grants Program (477)
income maintenance program (478)
welfare (479)

D. Overview of the Readings (pp. 487–494)

10.1. "Governor Perry's Fiscal Years 2004–2005 Budget: Two Opposing Views" (pp. 487–494)

This reading consists of two parts. In Part 10.1A, Republican governor Rick Perry defends his zero-based budget. In Part 10.1B, Representative Paul Moreno (D-El Paso) provides harsh criticism of the governor's action.

10.1A.   "Bottom Line on Why My Budget for Texas Starts at Zero" by Rick Perry (pp. 487–490)

In January 2003, Governor Perry submitted a zero-based budget to the Texas Legislature. Instead of recommending spending amounts for state agencies and their programs, Perry's budget had a zero for each item. He explains that this approach will require state agencies to "scrutinize their budgets line by line" and justify every expense. Instead of funding programs simply because an agency has received money in previous budgets, the governor insists that the legislature must focus on the core responsibilities of government and prioritize spending in order to balance the budget without tax increases or new taxes.

10.1B.   "Perry Gets Big Zero for Zero-Based Budget Ploy" by Paul Moreno (pp. 489–490)

Representative Paul Moreno takes Governor Perry to task for presenting the legislature with a budget calling for zero spending in every category—public education, higher education, teachers' health insurance, and all other functions of government. In brief, he criticizes Perry and other Republican leaders for action he describes as "grandstanding," "a stunt," a "political ploy." According to Moreno, Perry disregarded a provision of the Texas Constitution that requires the governor, "at the commencement of each regular session," to "present estimates of the amount of money required to be raised by taxation for all purposes." In conclusion, he faults Perry for lack of leadership and condemns the zero-based budget as "all symbol and zero substance."

10.2.   "Pediatrician Views Health Care Through Eyes of the Future" by Jeannie Kever (pp. 490–494)

At Houston's Ben Taub Hospital, pediatrician Ana Malinow daily comes face to face with the shortcomings of public health programs in Texas. She sees patients—children—whose parents have no other health care option. This leads some parents to wait until a problem becomes an emergency, to skimp on prescriptions that they cannot afford, and to burden the emergency room with such basic health care procedures as childhood vaccinations. While Malinow treats her young patients as well as the severely overburdened system allows, she also fights to change the system. She is co-founder of the Texas chapter of Health Care for All, an activist in the Green Party, and a volunteer at Casa Juan Diego, which serves a largely immigrant population. With 750,000 uninsured people in Harris County, or one of every 32 uninsured Americans, Malinow's goal of health care for all is a continuing struggle against great obstacles. But it a mission she has chosen.

II.   *Testing Your Knowledge*

A.   **True-False Questions on Text Material** (with textbook page numbers)

_____   10.1.   Since the adoption of the Texas Constitution of 1876, state fiscal policy has been dominated by the notion of a balanced budget. (440)

_____   10.2.   Texas has statutory and constitutional provisions requiring the state government to operate on a pay-as-you-go basis. (447)

_____   10.3.   For each regular session, the Legislative Budget Board and staff prepare a state budget and help the legislature draft a general appropriation bill. (451)

_____   10.4.   There are no limits on the budget-execution authority of the governor of Texas. (454)

_____   10.5.   The Council on Competitive Government measures the performance of Texas agencies against similar agencies in other state governments. (457)

_____   10.6.   Texas state government bases its financial operations on an accounting system whereby expenditures are entered when obligations are incurred rather than when money is actually paid. (457)

_____   10.7.   A government tax is a compulsory contribution for a public purpose. (458)

_____   10.8.   Texas sales taxes account for more than half of the state's annual tax revenue. (459)

_____   10.9.   Although Texas has a general sales tax, some items are exempted from taxation. (460)

_____   10.10.   Because the state relies heavily on revenues from sales taxes, Texas businesses have almost totally escaped state taxation. (462)

_____   10.11.   Texas taxpayers carry a tax burden that is lighter than the national average. (464)

_____   10.12.   Texas imposes a tax on horse-racing bets but *not* dog-racing bets. (465)

_____   10.13.   State governments are legally required to participate in all federal grant programs. (467)

_____   10.14.   Early in 1998, the American tobacco industry settled a lawsuit filed in 1996 by Governor George W. Bush. (469)

_____   10.15.   Although the Texas Constitution calls for pay-as-you-go financing of state government, bonded indebtedness has been authorized by constitutional amendments. (471)

_____ 10.16. Among Texas's self-liquidating bond issues is one that supports a college student loan fund. (471)

_____ 10.17. The Texas Tomorrow Funds allow prisoners to lock in the cost of cells and meals at prison units administered by the Texas Department of Criminal Justice. (477)

_____ 10.18. Direct payments for old-age assistance, aid to the blind, and aid to the permanently and totally disabled are the responsibility of the U.S. Social Security Administration. (479)

_____ 10.19. The Texas Department of Public Safety performs routine highway patrol functions and helps local law enforcement officers handle major crimes. (481)

_____ 10.20. Administrative costs of Texas state government amount to about 20 percent of the total. (482)

B.   True-False Questions on Readings (with textbook page numbers)

_____ 10.21. In January 2003, Governor Rick Perry gave the 78th Legislature a budget that provided for exactly the same amounts that had been appropriated for state agencies the 2002–2003 budget. (488)

_____ 10.22. Representative Paul Moreno charged that Governor Rick Perry's budgetary action in January 2003 failed to meet requirements of the Texas Constitution. (490)

_____ 10.23. Dr. Ana Malinow condemns Health Care for All as "failed socialism." (491)

_____ 10.24. About one in thirty-two Americans without health insurance live in the Houston area, which includes Harris and adjoining counties. (492)

C.   Multiple-Choice Questions on Text Material (with textbook page numbers)

_____ 10.25. Over the next few years, about 80 percent of nonagricultural employment in Texas will be provided by jobs in (441)

    a.   manufacturing.
    b.   construction.
    c.   oil and gas production.
    d.   the service sector.

_____ 10.26. Unless approved by a four-fifths vote in both houses of the Texas Legislature, an appropriation bill may not authorize the spending of more money than the cash on hand and revenue anticipated by the (447)

    a. treasurer.
    b. lieutenant governor.
    c. secretary of state.
    d. comptroller of public accounts.

_____ 10.27. Texans have demonstrated their greatest support for state spending for (449)

    a. welfare programs.
    b. recreational facilities.
    c. highways and roads.
    d. art and music.

_____ 10.28. In addition to receiving a plan of financial operation from the Legislative Budget Board, the Texas Legislature is supposed to receive another proposed budget from (451)

    a. the Judicial Budget Office.
    b. the Office of the State Treasurer.
    c. the Governor's Office of Budget, Planning and Policy.
    d. the Comptroller's Office.

_____ 10.29. Budget-preparation involves development of (452)

    a. itemized spending directives.
    b. an auditor's report.
    c. a tax proposal.
    d. a long-term strategic plan.

_____ 10.30. More than 90 percent of Texas's state taxes are collected by the (455)

    a. Department of Public Safety.
    b. Alcoholic Beverage Commission.
    c. State Board of Insurance.
    d. comptroller of public accounts.

_____ 10.31. The basic function of the state auditor is to provide the Texas Legislature with a check on the integrity and efficiency of (458)

    a. the executive branch of state government.
    b. the Legislative Budget Board.
    c. the judicial branch of state government.
    d. units of local government.

_____   10.32. For Texas state government, the most important single source of tax revenue is taxation on (459)

        a.   personal income.
        b.   sales.
        c.   real estate.
        d.   services.

_____   10.33. State taxes on cigarettes and other tobacco products, mixed drinks, and alcoholic beverages are called (461)

        a.   death taxes.
        b.   recreation taxes.
        c.   high-life taxes.
        d.   sin taxes.

_____   10.34. A payroll tax is levied for the purpose of insuring workers against (462)

        a.   illness.
        b.   foreign competition.
        c.   unemployment.
        d.   old age.

_____   10.35. The Texas crude oil production tax and the gas gathering tax are (463)

        a.   severance taxes.
        b.   motor fuel taxes.
        c.   income taxes.
        d.   sales taxes.

_____   10.36. All profits from the Texas lottery are dedicated to (466)

        a.   community colleges.
        b.   state universities.
        c.   public education.
        d.   Native American reservations.

_____   10.37. Under Texas law, bingo games are permitted for the purpose of benefiting (466)

        a.   charities.
        b.   professional gamblers.
        c.   children too young to bet on dogs and horses.
        d.   farmers and ranchers.

_____ 10.38. The tobacco settlement of 1998 is supposed to compensate for costs incurred by the state of Texas for tobacco-related (469)

    a. advertising.
    b. crime.
    c. drug abuse.
    d. illnesses.

_____ 10.39. Most of the money that has been invested by the state of Texas consists of (470)

    a. trust funds.
    b. a "rainy day" fund.
    c. political slush funds.
    d. federal grant-in-aid funds.

_____ 10.40. Sale of bonds is a way the state of Texas can (471)

    a. invest money.
    b. coin or print money.
    c. borrow money.
    d. obtain grants-in-aid.

_____ 10.41. Because it will be retired with loan repayments, a veterans land bond is classified as a (471)

    a. limited obligation bond.
    b. junk bond.
    c. self-liquidating revenue bond.
    d. general obligation bond.

_____ 10.42. Bonds issued by or on behalf of the state of Texas must be approved by (472)

    a. the comptroller of public accounts and the auditor.
    b. the governor and the secretary of state.
    c. the Legislative Budget Board.
    d. the Texas Bond Review Board.

_____ 10.43. Under Texas's Foundation School Program, each school system's local share—for the cost of salaries, transportation, and operating expenses—is based primarily on (475)

    a. the market value of taxable property in the school district.
    b. average daily attendance of pupils in the district.
    c. local economic conditions.
    d. types of students.

_____ 10.44. State financing for public community or junior colleges is based on hours of contact between (476)

    a. administrators and instructors.

    b. students and instructors.

    c. administrators and students.

    d. students and staff.

_____ 10.45. Revenue from Permanent University Fund investments is shared by (476)

    a. all public institutions of higher education in Texas.

    b. all public universities and technical colleges in Texas.

    c. all public universities in Texas.

    d. the University of Texas and Texas A&M University systems.

_____ 10.46. To meet one requirement for financial assistance through the Texas Grant program, a college or university student must (477)

    a. have graduated in the top 10 percent of his or her high school class.

    b. have a 3.5 GPA for his or her freshman year of higher education.

    c. be bilingual.

    d. show financial need.

_____ 10.47. Teach for Texas grants (converted to student loan repayment assistance by the 78th Legislature in 2003) were created for eligible students who teach after graduating for (478)

    a. 1 year.

    b. 3 years.

    c. 5 years.

    d. 10 years.

_____ 10.48. Texas leads the nation with the highest percentage of (480)

    a. undocumented immigrants.

    b. uninsured children.

    c. elderly persons.

    d. people with AIDS.

_____ 10.49. Texas's transportation policy encourages motor vehicle use to the detriment of other forms of transportation—especially (480)

    a. mass transit systems.

    b. bicycle riding in urban areas.

    c. hiking in rural areas.

    d. using boats and barges on rivers and canals.

10.50. Federal aid to states for their highway programs is dedicated primarily to (481)

    a. construction.
    b. maintenance.
    c. operating expenses.
    d. security.

10.51. The Texas Department of Criminal Justice operates (481)

    a. prison units and state felony jails.
    b. a law enforcement department.
    c. a court system.
    d. special schools and homes for juvenile delinquents.

D. Multiple-Choice Questions on Readings (with textbook page numbers)

10.52. Governor Rick Perry explains that his budget plan submitted to the 78th Legislature in January 2003 (487)

    a. starts at zero.
    b. covers functional expenditures.
    c. covers objective expenditures.
    d. is a "bare-bones" budget.

10.53. Representative Paul Moreno describes the budget submitted to the legislature by Governor Perry in 2003 as (490)

    a. extravagant and ill conceived.
    b. all symbol and zero substance.
    c. well intentioned but inadequate.
    d. something from "the pit of Hell."

10.54. Along with her hospital work in Houston, Dr. Ana Malinow is an assistant professor at (491)

    a. the University of Houston.
    b. Rice University.
    c. Cy-Fair Community College.
    d. Baylor College of Medicine.

_____   10.55. Dr. Ana Malinow, a pediatrician at Ben Taub Hospital, is an activist
in the (491)

    a. Libertarian Party.
    b. Democratic Party.
    c. Reform Party.
    d. Green Party.

E. Completion Questions on Text Material (with textbook page numbers)

10.56. Public policy that concerns taxes, government spending, public debt, and management of government money is termed _____ policy. (440)

10.57. The Robin Hood plan was designed to correct funding inequities between the
state's richest and poorest _____ districts. (442)

10.58. Although there are more than 400 funds in the Texas government's treasury, the
fund that is most crucial for the state's fiscal health is the _____
Revenue Fund. (447)

10.59. When there has been a need for more state revenue, Texans have indicated a
general preference for taxes that are classified as _____, because
the tax burden decreases as personal income increases. (448)

10.60. The fiscal management process in Texas state government begins with a budget
and ends with a(n) _____. (450)

10.61. The fiscal year for Texas state government begins on the first day of
_____. (450)

10.62. Each state agency requesting appropriated funds from the Texas Legislature
must submit a strategic operating plan to cover a period of _____ years.
(452)

10.63. Agencies of Texas state government must make purchases through or under the
supervision of the Texas Building and _____ Commission. (456)

10.64. Texas's general sales tax rate, 6.25 per cent, is one of the _____ in
the 45 states that have such a tax. (460)

10.65. An excise tax levied on a natural resource when it is removed from the earth is
called a _____ tax. (463)

10.66. The state of Texas collects a _____ percent tax on bingo prizes. (466)

10.67. Taxes amount to _____ than 50 percent of all Texas state revenue. (466)

10.68. To prevent or eliminate temporary cash deficiencies in the General Revenue Fund, the Texas Legislature established what is popularly called the "_____ day" fund. (472)

10.69. In general, the Foundation School Program sets minimum _____ for various areas of public school operations. (475)

10.70. Revenue raised locally by a school district is based primarily on the market value of taxable _____ within the district. (475)

10.71. Texas's *Lone Star Card* is used to deliver _____ stamp assistance to poor people who qualify for such aid. (479)

10.72. Historically, responsibility for protecting persons and property and for other public _____ programs was first delegated to local governments in Texas. (481)

F. Completion Questions on Readings (with textbook page numbers)

10. 73. Concerning state spending, Governor Rick Perry insists that vital state services must be provided without increasing the burden on Texas _____. (488)

10.74. Representative Paul Moreno disputes Governor Perry's contention that in making the state's budget, "_____ is on the table." (490)

10.75. Dr. Ana Malinow is one of the eight Texas members of _____ for a National Health Program. (492)

10.76. Dr. Ana Malinow describes her work as a pediatrician at Ben Taub Hospital as a _____. (494)

G. Essay Questions (with textbook page numbers)

1. Outline important changes in the Texas economy from the 1980s to early years of the twenty-first century, and explain how these changes have affected the state's fiscal policies. (440–442)
2. Identify and comment on Texas's enduring fiscal policy issues in the areas of public schools, highways, prisons, and welfare programs. (442–446)
3. Identify three basic principles that traditionally have shaped Texas fiscal policies, and comment on the consequences of these policies. (446–450)
4. Write an essay entitled "State Budgeting in Texas." Describe how the budget is prepared, how it is adopted, and how it is executed. Illustrate this budget process by drawing a diagram of the Texas budget process. (450–455)

5. Identify the Texas government agency that is most directly involved in each of the following functions: tax collection, lottery supervision, investment of public funds, state purchasing, accounting, and auditing state accounts. In addition, describe each function and explain its importance in giving Texans honest, efficient, economical government at the state level. (455–458)

6. Write an essay entitled "General and Selective Sales Taxes in Texas." Comment on their importance in terms of revenues produced and present arguments supporting *or* opposing any or all of these taxes. (458–462)

7. Write an essay entitled "Business Taxes in Texas." Identify the principal taxes, and explain the importance of each tax as a source of revenue and as a factor that influences the economic development of the state. (462–464)

8. Write an essay entitled "State Revenue from Gambling in Texas." In this essay, describe the forms of legalized gambling, and note the relative importance of state revenue from each. In conclusion, give arguments for and against legalization of each of these forms of gambling. (464–466)

9. Write an essay on "Nontax Revenue for the State of Texas." Describe sources of this revenue, and comment on the relative importance of each source for balancing the state budget. (466–470)

10. Write an essay entitled "The State Government's Public Debt in Texas." Explain how the state has acquired a debt despite the Texas Constitution's "pay-as-you-go" requirement, and give arguments for and against state borrowing by issuing bonds. (470–472)

11. Using public schools (kindergarten through high school) *or* public higher education (community colleges, state universities, and state technical colleges) as your subject, write an essay in which you discuss recent problems and achievements in financing Texas governmental operations in that area. (474–478)

12. Using data in the How Do We Compare box at the top of page 461 of this chapter, rank the eight states in descending order according to amount of revenue lost from Internet sales in 2001. How does Texas rank?

13. Using data in the How Do We Compare box at the top of page 473 of this chapter, rank the eight states in descending order according to per capita expenditure for education in FY2000. How does Texas rank?

III. Applying Your Knowledge

A. Outside Readings and Cartoons

1. From the endnotes for this chapter or from the updated bibliography of selected sources accessible through the Houghton Mifflin Political Science

home page (politicalscience.college.hmco.com), choose a magazine article or journal article and write a summary of it.

2. From the endnotes for this chapter of from the updated bibliography of selected sources accessible through the Houghton Mifflin Political Science home page (politicalscience.college.hmco.com), choose a book and write a summary of one of its chapters.
3. In a newspaper, find an editorial concerning state fiscal policy. Summarize that editorial, and explain why you agree or disagree with the writer's point of view.
4. Find a newspaper article concerning state fiscal policy. Summarize the article, and describe what you do and/or do not like about this piece of reporting.
5. Interpret one of this chapter's cartoons (or another cartoon) concerning state fiscal policy, and explain why you agree or disagree with the cartoonist's point of view.
6. Explore two or more of the web sites listed among sources for this chapter. Then select one site and write a brief note outlining how its information contributes to your understanding of state fiscal policy.

B.   Internet Research Project

Objectives

1. To increase student understanding of the role of the Office of the Comptroller of Public Accounts in the state budgetary process.
2. To familiarize students with the changing sources of state revenue.
3. To enhance student awareness of state spending priorities.
4. To become aware of the free publications provided by the Office of the Comptroller.
5. To further increase student understanding of distinctions between search engines and directories and the use of parallel search services.

URL. http://www.window.state.tx.us

Description of the Site. The Research Division of the Office of the Comptroller of Public Accounts is responsible for providing information to the Texas Legislature on the financial condition of the state at the end of each fiscal year. Every two years, when the legislature is in regular session, it must also prepare estimates of projected revenue for the legislature's use in preparing the biennial state budget. This information is critical to the state budgeting process. The Texas Constitution mandates that the legislature can only spend as much money as the comptroller has certified will be available.

This web site is maintained by the Office of the Comptroller of Public Accounts and includes the required biennial revenue estimate. It also contains historical information on Texas's economy. State spending for each fiscal year since 1978 is categorized by governmental function. Sources of state revenue are identified, and the dollar amount produced by each type of income is provided.

The Internet is a dynamic, ever-changing environment. If any of the links and instructions need to be adjusted please consult the textbook website for updates of this exercise (http://college.hmco.com/polisci/brown/prac_tex_pol/12e/students/index.html).

Use of Information. For this exercise, you will review state revenue, state spending, and the most recent Biennial Revenue Estimate prepared by the Office of the Comptroller. Based on this information, you are to answer a series of questions.

1. Go to the comptroller's home page (http://www.window.state.tx.us).

2. Locate the "Quick Links" list. Click on the hyperlink "Site Map." This will take you to an index of all topics available at this site.

3. Click on the hyperlink "Texas Taxes."

4. Scroll to the subsection called "Revenue and Budget." The most recent "Biennial Revenue Estimate," "Texas Revenue History by Source," and "Texas Expenditure History by Function" are all listed in hypertext in this subsection.

5. Click on "Texas Revenue History by Source." You should now be on the page that identifies Texas's revenue by source beginning with the most current year.

6. Scroll to "Revenue by Source—Fiscal 1990." Identify the top three sources of income to the state by percentage of total income in 1990, Rank these sources, listing them and their percent of total income.

    (1) _____
    (2) _____
    (3) _____

7. Scroll back to the top of the page. Identify the top three sources of income to the state by percentage of total income for the most recent year available, and rank them. List them and their percent of total income.

    (1) _____
    (2) _____
    (3) _____

8. What changes have there been in the top sources of income since 1990?

    _____

    _____

9. The oil and gas industries were once a major source of revenue for the state. Sum the percent of state revenue that came from "Natural Gas Production Tax" and "Oil Production and Regulation Taxes" for 1978. Do the same for 1990 and for the most recent year. Report these data below:

    a. _____

    b. _____

    c. _____

    What trend do you see in the importance of oil and gas taxes for state revenues?

    _____

    _____

10. Click on the "Back" icon to return to the Site Map. Scroll down to "Tax and Budget," and click on "Texas Expenditure History by Function." This page also begins with the most recent year's information and extends back to 1978.

11. Scroll to "Expenditures by Function—Fiscal 1990." Identify the state's top five spending categories by percentage of total expenditures in 1990 and rank them. List them and their percent of total income.

    (1) _____

    (2) _____

    (3) _____

    (4) _____

    (5) _____

12. Scroll up the page to the most recent fiscal year. Identify the state's top five spending categories by percentage of total expenditures, and rank them. List them and their percent of total income.

    (1) _____

    (2) _____

    (3) _____

    (4) _____

    (5) _____

13. If the amount of money legislators are willing to spend on a category of governmental goods and services reflects how important that good or service is to the citizens of Texas, what trends can you identify in state spending priorities since 1990?

_____

_____

_____

_____

14. Click on the "Back" icon to return to the "Site Map." Scroll to "Revenue and Budget." Click on the most recent "Biennial Revenue Estimate." Scroll down to the "Revenue Overview" hyperlink and click on it. How much money does the comptroller believe will be available for general spending by the legislature over that biennium?

_____

15. Go to the bottom of the page and click on the hyperlink "Window on State Government." You are now back on the Comptroller's homepage. Click on "Publications." Here you can see there are many articles dealing with Education, Economy, State Government, Local Government, and Revenue and the Budget.

16. There is also a list of Periodicals published by the state. Click on "Fiscal Notes." Then click on the link "On-line Subscription Form." Scroll down the form to the list of publications to which you can subscribe <u>for free</u>. What are the titles of the first three publications listed?

a. _____

b. _____

c. _____

Internet Research Tip. Information on the Internet is so vast and growing at such a rapid pace that the use of search engines and directories is required to conduct efficient research. Generally, these research tools connect only to the World Wide Web, although some do connect to other Internet resources. A search engine is a computer program that can search a database of Internet resources. Computer programs that search the Internet to identify and catalogue sites often compile it. Examples of search engines include AltaVista <http://altavista.digital.com>, Excite <http://www.excite.com>, and WebCrawler <http://www.webcrawler.com>.

Researchers and editors who select Web pages they believe to be useful compile directories. This information is then indexed by subject categories. Examples of directories include Yahoo! <http://www.yahoo.com>, Magellan <http://www.mckinley.com/>, and Google <http://www.google. com/>. Search engines and directories are becoming more similar, as both query-driven and subject-driven searches can often be conducted on either.

As noted in Chapter 3 of this *Study Guide,* for more complete results a user should perform both query-driven and subject-driven searches on a number of search engines and directories. It is possible to conduct parallel searches on both search engines and directories by using a search service such as MetaCrawler <http://www.metacrawler.com>. MetaCrawler does not maintain its own database. It submits requests to a number of services and directories. This method gives the user simultaneous access to multiple databases. Responses are returned to MetaCrawler, which then formats them and rates them according to relevancy. Combining the relevancy scores provided by the different engines and directories for each site or page, MetaCrawler then ranks the sites and returns them to the user. Although MetaCrawler is slower than other search engines, consider how long it would take to conduct multiple individual searches by going to each of the services and directories accessed by MetaCrawler

Answers

True-False: Text	Multiple-Choice: Text	Multiple-Choice: Readings
10.1. T	10.25. d	10.52. a
10.2. T	10.26. d	10.53. b
10.3. T	10.27. c	10.54. d
10.4. F	10.28, c	10.55. d
10.5. F	10.29. d	
10.6. F	10.30. d	**Completion: Text**
10.7. T	10.31. a	
10.8. T	10.32. b	10.56. fiscal
10.9. T	10.33. d	10.57. school
10.10. F	10.34. c	10.58. General
10.11. T	10.35. a	10.59. regressive
10.12. F	10.36. c	10.60. audit
10.13. F	10.37. a	10.61. September
10.14. F	10.38. d	10.62. five
10.15. T	10.39. a	10.63. Procurement
10.16. T	10.40. c	10.64. highest
10.17. F	10.41. c	10.65. severance
10.18. T	10.42. d	10.66. 5
10.19. T	10.43. a	10.67. less
10.20. F	10.44. b	10.68. rainy
	10.45. d	10.69. standards
True-False: Readings	10.46. d	10.70. property
	10.47. c	10.71. food
10.21. F	10.48. b	10.72. safety
10.22. T	10.49. a	
10.23. F	10.50. a	**Completion: Readings**
10.24. T	10.51. a	
		10.73. taxpayers
		10.74. everything
		10.75. Physicians
		10.76. mission